LAW

A TREATISE

BY

NŪR-UD-DĪN ʿABD-UR-RAḤMĀN JĀMĪ

(FACSIMILE OF AN OLD MS.)

WITH A TRANSLATION BY

E. H. WHINFIELD, M.A., & MĪRZĀ MUḤAMMAD ḲAZVĪNĪ

AND PREFACE ON THE
INFLUENCE OF GREEK PHILOSOPHY UPON SŪFISM

Reprinted with Additions and Corrections

NEW INTRODUCTION BY
SEYYED HOSSEIN NASR
Director, Imperial Iranian Academy of Philosophy

THEOSOPHICAL PUBLISHING HOUSE LTD
LONDON

ADYAR, MADRAS   WHEATON ILLINOIS

INDIA   U.S.A.

© Royal Asiatic Society, London

LAWAIH, Oriental Translation Fund, New Series Vol **XVI**
published in 1928, and reprinted in its entirety by the **Theo**-
sophical Publishing House Ltd, 68 Great Russell Street, **London**
WC1B 3BU, 1978. No part of this publication may be reproduced
in any form without permission from the copyright holder.

ISBN 7229 5135 3 hardback
ISBN 7229 5136 1 paperback

First Edition	1906
Second Edition	1914
Reprinted	1928
Reprinted	1978

Printed in Great Britain by
Fletcher & Son Ltd, Norwich

CONTENTS

See but One, say but One, know but One.

Gulshān i Rāz, 1. 883.

The *Alif* of the Loved One's form is graven on my heart,
No other letter did my Shaikh ever to me impart.

Ḥāfiẓ, Ode 416 (ed. Brockhaus).

My heart inquired, " What is the heaven-sent lore ?
If thou'st attained it, teach me, I implore."
  "*Alif*," I said, "if there be one within,
One letter serves to name him—say no more."

OMAR KHAYYĀM, Quatrain 109.

PREFACE TO THE 1906 EDITION

THE *Lawā'iḥ* is a treatise on Ṣūfī theology or theosophy, as distinguished from the religious emotions experienced by all Ṣūfīs, learned and unlearned alike. Catholic authorities have drawn this distinction between "experimental" and "doctrinal" mysticism,[1] and it is a great help towards clear thinking on this subject. The religious emotion common to all mankind is, so to speak, raised to its highest power in the mystics. They are overwhelmed by the sense of the Divine omnipresence and of their own dependence on God. They are dominated and intoxicated by their vivid sense of the close relation subsisting between the soul and God. They conceive themselves as being in touch with God, feeling His motions in their souls, and at times rising to the beatific vision and blinded by excess of light. These religious experiences were the rough material out of which the doctrinal reasoned system, set out in treatises like the *Lawā'iḥ*, was built up. Psychologists have advanced various theories as to the genesis of these experiences.[2] With these we are not at present concerned. But as to the origin of the philosophical ideas and terms employed in the *Lawā'iḥ* and similar works to formulate the Ṣūfī theology, there can be little doubt. The source of Ṣūfī theology was Neoplatonism.

The title of the book, *Lawā'iḥ*, or "Flashes of Light", suggests the philosophy employed to systematize and give

[1] See the article on "Mystical Theology" in Addis & Arnold's *Catholic Dictionary*.

[2] See Dr. William James's *Varieties of Religious Experience* (Longmans, 1902). It may be doubted whether the "subliminal self" affords a satisfactory solution of the problem.

a reasoned basis for the unreasoned "experiences" of unlearned Ṣūfīs. It of course refers to the "inner light". The Platonists were called *Ishrāqīn* or *Illuminati*, because they regarded intellectual intuition or intuitive reason (*Nous*) as the main source of knowledge, whereas the Peripatetics (*Mashshā'īn*) recognized no sources of knowledge except the senses and the discursive reason (*Dianoia*). The word *Ishrāq*, or "Lights", is often met with in this connexion. Thus Shams-ud-dīn Muḥammad ash-Shahrazūrī is called by Haji Khalfa "a metaphysician learned in the inner lights" (*Ishrāq*).[1] Shihāb-ud-dīn as Suhrawardī, who was put to death at Aleppo in 587 A.H. by advice of that valiant defender of the Faith, Sulṭān Ṣalāḥ-ud-dīn, wrote a book entitled *Ḥikmat-ul-Ishrāq*, or "Philosophy of Inner Light".[2] The author of the *Dabistān* says that the belief of the pure Ṣūfīs is the same as that of the *Ishrāqīn* or Platonists,[3] and also that Ṣūfīs were classed as orthodox (*Mutasharri'*) and Platonists.[4] Haji Khalfa, in his article on Ṣūfism (*Taṣawwuf*), says that anyone who reads Ṣūfī books cannot fail to remark that their terminology is borrowed from the Platonists (*Ishrāqīn*), and more especially from the later ones—i.e. the Neoplatonists.[5] Let any reader who has even a slight acquaintance with the terms used by the Greek philosophers look over treatises like the *Lawā'iḥ* and the *Gulshan i Rāz* and on almost every page he will recognize some familiar Greek term. Schmölders in his *Documenta Philosophiæ Arabum* gives a list of nearly one hundred such terms employed by Avicena (Ibn Sīna) and other writers on philosophy in the fifth century of the Hijira.

[1] Haji Khalfa, iii, 479.

[2] Ibn Khallikan, iv, 153. This Shihāb-ud-dīn must not be confounded with his more famous namesake who died at Baghdad in the odour of sanctity in 632 A.H. Ibn Khallikan, ii, 382.

[3] Shea & Troyer's translation, iii, 281.

[4] Ibid. ii, 374 ; see also iii, 139.   [5] Haji Khalfa, ii, 308.

It was probably at about the end of the fifth century A.H. that Neoplatonic *gnōsis* began to influence and modify Ṣūfī doctrine. Up to that date the doctrine had been expounded in short precepts, parables (*mithāl*), and similes like those in the Koran. But educated Moslems had outgrown these primitive methods of instruction. They wanted something more systematic. Jalāl-ud-dīn Rūmī tells us how his critics assailed him for dealing in trivial examples and parables instead of giving a systematic account of the stages of the soul's ascent to God.[1] Ibn Khaldūn mentions Muḥāsibī and the great Imām Ghazālī as among the first who wrote systematic treatises on the doctrines of the Ṣūfīs.[2] We have Ghazālī's own account of the way in which he was attracted to Ṣūfism,[3] and other passages in his writings prove that he used the forms of Greek thought to explain Ṣūfī principles.[4] If it be asked how Greek philosophy reached Ghazālī, who was a native of Khurāsān,[5] the answer is easy. When Justinian closed the schools at Athens, Damascius and his Neoplatonist brethren fled to the court of Nushirvān. They only remained there about a year, and left in 533 A.D.; but Nushirvān had some translations of Neoplatonist books made at the time, and these were followed by many others, made two centuries and a half later, under the Abbasides at Baghdad.[6]

Greek philosophy was expounded by the so-called Arabian, but really Persian, philosophers, Al Farābī and Avicena, and afterwards in the *Ikhwān-uṣ-Ṣafā*.[7] Shahrastānī, a contemporary of Ghazālī, gave accounts

[1] See *Masnavī*, p. 168.

[2] *Notices et Extraits des Manuscrits*, xii, 301, 302.

[3] See Schmölders' *Écoles Philosophiques chez les Arabes*, p. 55.

[4] See Appendix I.

[5] Khurāsān was the "focus of culture", as Hammer says, and many of the philosophers came from that Eastern province.

[6] Whittaker's *Neoplatonists*, p. 133; and Schmölders' *Documenta Philosophiæ Arabum* (Bonn, 1836), Introduction.

[7] See Dieterici's *Die Weltseele* (Leipzig, 1872).

of all the chief Greek philosophers, including the
"Shaikh of the Greeks" or Plotinus,[1] his editor Porphyry,
and Proclus. The so-called "Theology of Aristotle",
which is a summary of the "Enneads" of Plotinus,[2]
appeared probably soon afterwards. The result was that
Neoplatonism, mainly in the form expounded by Plotinus,
was used by all the more learned Ṣūfīs to explain and
justify the simple emotional sayings of the early Ṣūfīs.
Henceforward Neoplatonism pervades all systematic
treatises on Ṣūfism, such as the *Faṣūṣ-ul-Ḥikam*, the
Maqṣad-ul-Aqṣā,[3] the *Gulshan i Rāz*,[4] and the *Lawā'iḥ*.
Even the poets use the Greek terminology. Thus Ḥakīm
Sanā'ī, who lived at the same time as Ghazālī, introduces
"Universal Reason" and "Universal Soul", the second
and third hypostases of the Trinity of Plotinus, and the
principal later poets follow suit.[5]

The first Ṣūfīs differed from ordinary Moslems only in
their quietism (*taslīm*) and their puritan ideal of life.
They held the orthodox doctrines, with perhaps a few
reservations. But when Greek influences came into play
all these doctrines underwent more or less modification.
Take the following samples :—

1. The central doctrine of Islām, "There is no God but
Allah," was "restated" in the form "There is no real
Being and no real Agent (*Fā'il i ḥaqīqī*) but the One,
'The Truth' (*Al Ḥaqq*)". Allah was not entirely stripped
of personal attributes such as will and consciousness, but

---

[1] See Haarbrücker's German translation of Shahrastānī's *Book of Sects*,
ii, 192 (Halle, 1850).

[2] See Dr. Brönnle's note, Journal of the Royal Asiatic Society, April,
1901. The book was published with a Latin translation by Petrus
Nicolaus in 1518.

[3] The late Professor Palmer published a summary of this book under
the title of *Oriental Mysticism* (Cambridge, 1867).

[4] Edited and translated by me (Trübner, 1880).

[5] Mr. Nicholson has brought this out in his *Dīwāni Shamsi Tabrīz*
(Cambridge, 1898). For a sketch of the system of Plotinus see
Appendix II.

He has ceased to be conceived as a purely supramundane Deity, enthroned above the empyrean heaven, creating the world by one fiat, ruling His subjects, like some mighty monarch, by commands and prohibitions, and paying them wages according to their deserts. He has become a Being immanent and "deeply interfused" in the universe,[1] and giving it all the real existence it has. The Koran speaks of Allah as omniscient, but omniscience was now expanded into "omni-essence", if one may use such a word.[2] It was the Plotinian doctrine of the "One" and its Emanations which furnished the Sūfī theologians with the material for this wider conception of "The Truth", the ultimate divine ground of all things, the "Substance" as Spinoza called it.

2. Like all great religious teachers, Muhammad laid chief stress on right conduct, and this consisted in implicit obedience to every one of Allah's commands, as disobedience to any one was sin. The distinction between moral laws and commands merely relating to ritual observances was not clearly laid down. It has been said that Islām means "striving after righteousness".[3] That is so, but righteousness was interpreted as including the scrupulous observance of trivial rules as to ablutions,

---

[1] Cf. Wordsworth, "Lines on Tintern Abbey"—

> "A sense sublime
> Of something far more deeply interfused,
> Whose dwelling is the light of setting suns,
> And the round ocean and the living air,
> And the blue sky, and in the heart of man ;
> A motion and a spirit that impels
> All thinking things, all objects of all thought,
> And rolls through all things."

[2] "Or omneity," as Sir Thomas Browne calls it in the *Religio Medici*, § 35.

[3] Surah lxxii, 14 ; Hirschfeld, p. 14 ; and Suhrawardy's *Sayings of Muhammad*. Jorjānī defines Islām as unquestioning obedience and submission to Allah's commands (*Notices et Extraits des Manuscrits*, **x,** 53).

prayers, fasting, etc.[1] It may well be doubted **if**
Muhammad is responsible for some of the directions
about ritual which are ascribed to him,[2] but, be this **as**
it may, more and more importance came to be assigned **to**
the scrupulous observance of these ritual forms. The
early Ṣūfīs, like the Quakers, held that divine illumination
and grace were imparted directly to every soul, and **not**
through the channel of external observances. They
thought that the mechanical routine of rites (*taqlīd*)
only served to induce the spiritual torpor which Dante
called "accidia".[3] St. Bernard remarked this result in
his monks, but he set it down to the fault of the men, not
to that of the system. The Ṣūfī theologians adopted the
Neoplatonist view that the ritual law is not binding upon
spiritual men. In like manner St. Paul called the Jewish
law a "yoke of bondage" (*taqlīd*). Shabistarī contrasts
the mere outward Islām of ritual observances with the
true piety of some heathens, much to the advantage of
the latter, and Jalāl-ud-dīn Rūmī declares that "Fools
exalt the Mosque while they ignore the true temple in
the heart".[4]

3. Greek philosophy taught the immortality of the
soul, but denied the resurrection of the body. And hence
the language of the Koran about Heaven and Hell
ultimately came to be regarded as merely allegorical.
The early Ṣūfīs held very strongly that love to God
should be quite disinterested and untainted by hope of

---

[1] See the rules about ablution, etc., in the *Mishcāt ul Maṣābiḥ*,
translated by Matthews (Calcutta, 1809). Cf. Omar Khayyām's
"whimsical complaint", Quatrain 180.

[2] They seem opposed to the spirit of the text : " Righteousness does
not consist in turning to the east or to the west," etc. (Surah ii, 172).

[3] " Purgatory " (canto xvii). From the Greek *akēdeia*.

[4] *Gulshan i Rāz*, l. 877 ; and *Masnavī*, p. 100, and Introduction,
p. xxxiv (2nd ed.). But elsewhere (at p. 76) Jalāl-ud-dīn says forms and
symbols are generally needed. In default of some outward and visible
sign which they can *perceive*, men find it hard to *conceive* the inward
spirit. Hence the Greek mystics in their "mysteries" used sacraments
or outward forms of initiation and communion.

reward. They thought "other-worldliness" no better than worldliness. According to the Ṣūfī theologians there is no material heaven or hell. When the particle of real being in each soul is stripped of its mortal vesture, "of what account" (they asked) "will be Paradise and houris?"[1] In the case of those who have retained a perfect reasonable soul the divine particle will return intact to the One Real Being. When the soul has in life shrunk to a mere animal or vegetive soul, some remnant of the divine particle within it may still survive and return to the One Being. But if the divine spark has been utterly quenched by evil living there is nothing left which can survive. Dr. Charles in his *Eschatology* says that some Jewish apocalyptic writers held that there was no resurrection of the wicked.

4. Muḥammad had no taste for speculation. He said : "Think on the mercies of God, not on the essence of God." And again : "Sit not with those who discuss predestination." His language on predestination is merely popular. In one passage it is that of determinism, in another that of freewill. In one place Allah constrains all, guiding some aright and causing others to err.[2] Elsewhere man acts freely without constraint. But the theologians fastened on these obscure problems, and did their best to shift the religious centre of gravity from right conduct to right opinion on these problems. In a word they preached salvation by *gnōsis*. The traditionists fathered on Muḥammad various sayings to prove that he regarded orthodoxy on these "afterthoughts of theology" as all-important for salvation. Thus the saying "My people shall be split into seventy-three sects, all of whom but one shall perish in hell fire" is one which betrays theological authorship. In Muḥammad's lifetime the contest was not with sects within Islām, but with aliens who rejected Islām altogether. For these he had no mercy, but he

---

[1] *Gulshan i Rāz*, l. 701. [2] Koran, xvi, 38, 39.

would scarcely have been so hard on his own people for venial errors of opinion. Again, he could hardly have said "Qadarians are Magian (dualists)" at a time when (as is almost certain) no sect of that name had yet arisen.[1] The early Ṣūfīs did not concern themselves with the disputes of the sects. But the Ṣūfī theologians could not altogether ignore them. They took sides against the sects which leaned to anthropomorphism, and, on the other hand, fully agreed with the doctrine of the Compulsionists or extreme Predestinarians.[2] That sect held that God, as the One Real Agent, not only permitted evil, but of set purpose allotted evils, present or future, to the majority of mankind. This strange doctrine (which has its counterpart in Europe) forced the Ṣūfī theologians to attempt some reconciliation of Divine power, as thus interpreted, with Divine goodness, and here, like Augustine, they availed themselves of the "not-being" (*'adm*) of Plotinus.[3]

Perhaps, however, the true Ṣūfī spirit was best interpreted by Jalāl-ud-dīn Rūmī, when he declared that he agreed with all seventy-three sects as being all honest attempts to grasp the obscure truth. Errors in "naming the names of God" are of small account. According to the *Ḥadīth*, "He who does the works will know the doctrine." And true love to God atones for all mistakes of doctrine.[4]

Jāmī is a typical Ṣūfī theologian. He works hard to construct a reasoned basis for Ṣūfism, but finally realizes that his logical definitions and syllogisms cannot express the truth as it really is, and add nothing to the grounds

---

[1] The Qadarians would be classed as semi-Pelagians by Western theologians.

[2] See *Gulshan i Rāz*, ll. 105, 538.

[3] See *Masnavī* (2nd ed.), Introduction, p. xxx, etc., and Flash XXVII in this treatise.

[4] See the parable of Moses and the shepherd who was faulty in theology but fervent in spirit (*Masnavī*, p. 82, and also p. 139).

on which the convictions of Ṣūfīs must always rest. It
is only by means of the spiritual clairvoyance generated
by love that Divine knowledge (*maʻrifat*) can be attained.[1]
Those who have these spiritual intuitions do not need
demonstrations, and to those who have them not all
demonstrations are useless.

5. Muḥammad, like Luther, rejected asceticism. Suhrawardy quotes several of his anti-ascetic sayings, including
the familar one " There is no monasticism in Islām ". He
approved of poverty, it is true, and prescribed a month of
fasting, but set his face firmly against the cloistered life
and celibacy.[2] The early Ṣūfīs were, perhaps, attracted
to asceticism by the example of the Christians in Syria,
where the first Ṣūfī convent was built ; and Neoplatonist
doctrine furnished the rationale of ascetic practice. Matter
was evil, and therefore all material and sensuous taint,
including the natural instincts (*phronēma sarkos*), must
be purged away and extirpated by all who claimed to be
spiritual men.[3] Thus a double system of religious conduct
was set up—the external law for ordinary men and " the
counsels of perfection", the mo· ᵣ perfect way of asceticism
and contemplation, for spiritual men. The external law
of ritual observances had no longer any dominion over
spiritual men.[4] This abrogation of the ceremonial law
naturally tempted some undisciplined Ṣūfīs, as it has
tempted some professing followers of St. Paul, to laxity
in the observance of the moral law. The Malāmatīs,

[1] See *Masnavī*, p. 260. Newman (*Apologia*, p. 19) quotes Keble as
saying, " The firmness of assent which we give to religious doctrine
is due, not to the probabilities which introduced it, but to the living
power of faith and love which accepted it." This is worked out in
Newman's *Grammar of Assent*.

[2] See the *Sayings of Muḥammad*, by Suhrawardy (Constable, 1905),
Nos. 125, 304, 186, etc.

[3] Jalāl-ud-dīn Rūmī, however, takes occasion to warn his disciples
that this counsel of perfection is not to be taken too literally. See the
parable of the peacock who tore off his plumage to avoid the pursuit of
the fowlers (*Masnavī*, p. 228).

[4] See *Masnavī*, p. 224.

for instance, committed immoral acts in order to court reproach and humble their self-esteem. But such doctrines were always condemned by the more authoritative Ṣūfī theologians. Thus Shabistarī (*Gulshan i Rāz*, Answer iv) says that the true mystic who has attained "union" must not rest in that ecstatic state, but while he is in the flesh must journey down again, wearing the law as his outer garment and carrying out its obligations.

6. The Ṣūfī "Contemplation" (*Mushāhadah*) is closely allied to the Plotinian "deifying virtue" of *Theōria* explained as *Theou orasis* or the beatific vision. One line of scholars, led by A. von Kremer, however, traces this element of Ṣūfism to Vedantism or to Buddhism. The objections to this view are first that no Indian terms are found in Ṣūfī writings and secondly that the Buddhist *Nirvāna* is an end in itself; the Ṣūfī *Fanā* is only the preliminary to *Baqā*, continued existence in the One Real Being. When the One becomes the "heir of all", or, as St. Paul says, when He is "all in all" (*panta en pasin*), Ṣūfīs look for an immortality of an impersonal character, concentrated in the One. Lastly, *metempsychōsis* is condemned by Ṣūfī theologians (*Gulshan i Rāz*, l. 106).

Harnack, in his *History of Dogma*, has shown how profoundly Christian theology has been affected by Neoplatonist ideas. The disputes about *Ousia*, *Hypostasis*, and *Physis* which rent Christendom asunder [1] mainly grew from "afterthoughts of theology" suggested by these ideas, and their influence has extended to our own days.[2] It is hardly too much to say that their influence on the course of events has been as considerable as that of the Roman law. In Islām their influence has

[1] Gibbon's *Decline and Fall*, ch. xxi.

[2] "Paulus genuit Augustinum et Augustinus genuit Calvinum." With Paul should be coupled Plotinus. See Bigg's Introduction to *Augustine's Confessions* (Methuen, 1903).

been much more restricted than in Christendom, but, such as it was, it is instructive to trace it.[1]

The manuscript of the *Lawā'iḥ* now reproduced is undated, but was probably written within a century of Jāmī's death in 898 A.H. It once belonged to the royal library at Delhi, and the outside pages contain notes by the librarians, one of which, dated the 24th year of Aurangzīb, states that it was worm-eaten even then. W. H. Morley, who also owned it, has noted on the fly-leaf his opinion that it is not Jāmī's work, but written by one Sayyid 'Abd ul Kāfi. This, however, is certainly a mistake. Haji Khalfa, in his notice of Jāmī's *Lawā'iḥ*, quotes the beginning, which agrees with the beginning of this manuscript,[2] and one of the quatrains gives Jāmī's name. The British Museum possesses three copies—viz., Add. 16820 (Rieu, p. 44*a*); Add. 16819, iv (Rieu, p. 826*b*) ; and Add. 7689, iv, fol. 150 onwards (Rieu, p. 810*b*). Copies are to be found in other libraries. In addition to that now reproduced, I possess one, written in an Indian hand, probably in the eighteenth century.[3]

The facsimile of the manuscript has been made by Messrs. Nops, of Ludgate Hill. They have been very successful in removing nearly all traces of the stains and worm-holes in the original, and I think the writer of the manuscript himself, could he see it, would find little fault with their reproduction of his handiwork.

I began the translation some years ago, but, owing to failing eyesight, had to stop after getting to the end of Flash VII. I have now been fortunate enough to secure the assistance of a very competent scholar, Mīrzā Muḥammad Ḳazvīnī, who has furnished me with a literal

[1] For a sketch of the system of Plotinus, who is the best exponent of Neoplatonism, see Appendix II.

[2] Haji Khalfa, v, 344.

[3] The Munich Catalogue, p. 21, mentions a manuscript of the *Lawāyih* [*sic*] with a different beginning.

French version of the whole, together with some valuable
notes. In his translation the Mīrzā has chiefly followed
the British Museum Manuscript Add. No. 16819, which
contains several passages not found in this manuscript.
Most, if not all, of these seem to me to be glosses which
have crept into the text, but I have given them in this
translation, marking them with square brackets. Up to
the end of Flash VII the accompanying translation is
that made by me some years ago, with some corrections
suggested by the Mīrzā's version. From the beginning of
Flash VIII to the end of the book the translation is the
Mīrzā's French version turned into English by me. In
this part of the work I have followed the Mīrzā closely,
only referring to the original to verify a word here and
there. I am solely responsible for the Preface and notes.
If they contain errors of fact or doctrine, these must not
be imputed to the Mīrzā.

The references to the *Gulshan i Rāz* are to my edition
of that work (Trübner, 1880); those to the *Masnavī* of
Jalāl-ud-dīn Rūmī to my translation of that poem (second
edition, published in Trübner's Oriental Series, 1898);
those to Omar Khayyām to my text and translation,
published in the same series, second edition, 1901.

As regards transliteration, I follow the rule laid down
long since by the Indian Government, that when foreign
words have become naturalized in English they should be
spelled according to English usage. Thus I write Calcutta,
Moslem, Koran, Abbasides, etc. Again, when a Persian
writer has chosen to transliterate his own name in a
particular way, I do not presume to interfere with his
discretion. I give titles of books as they are spelled on
the title-pages, and, like Rieu, I represent *hamza* by the
"spiritus lenis" ('). With these exceptions I have in the
main observed the transliteration rules of the Royal
Asiatic Society.

E. H. W.

In the Name of God, Most Merciful, Most
Compassionate

INTRODUCTION TO THE NEW EDITION
by
Seyyed Hossein Nasr

Over seventy years after the first printing of the text and
English translation of the *Lawā'ih* of Jāmī, this short but
precious summary of Sufi doctrine is being printed once
again. During this period, genuine studies of Sufism have
appeared in Western languages, and a few in the Occident
have begun to take Sufism and other forms of authentic
esoteric doctrines more seriously than when Whinfield
began his translation of the *Lawā ih*, although optical
illusions and deformations by many orientalists continue
to linger in academic circles. Despite these distorted and
truncated interpretations of Sufism, however, it is now
possible to discuss Sufism from its own point of view and
in serious terms in the West in a manner that was not possible for the scholars of the turn of the century, who had,
for the most part, no access to either authentic Sufi teachings or similar traditional doctrines belonging to other
sources. Faced on the one hand with theology in its most
restricted form, and on the other with various types of
occultism or bland syncretisms without serious foundation,
most of the scholars of this early period could not quite
" situate " a doctrine such as that of Sufism. They
therefore, took recourse to comparing it with, and even
reducing it to, a philosophical pantheism or monism
usually purported to be of Neoplatonic origin and there-

fore of little significance and devoid of authenticity,[1] or a
harmless " idealism " in the manner of the German and
Anglo-Saxon schools of philosophical idealism in the late
19th century. The sacred character of metaphysics, its
attachment to spiritual practice, the saving quality of the
illuminated intellect and the grace which is associated
with Sufi doctrine were forgotten even if translations were
made into fairly elegant English and a service thus ren-
dered to making the treasures of Sufism known in the
West.   It is, therefore, appropriate to lay aside the earlier
interpretations and view the *Lawā'ih* and its author once
again from the perspective of Sufism itself.

The celebrated Persian poet, Nūr al-Dīn 'Abd al-
Rahmān Jāmī was born near Herat in 817/1414 in a family
which had migrated there from Isfahan.   He studied in
the city of his birth and soon mastered all the traditional
sciences from mathematics and astronomy to philosophy
and theology and became a renowned scholar.   He also
was deeply attracted to Sufism and became a devout disciple of Sa'd al-Dīn Muhammad Kāshghārī who was himself linked through two generations of masters to Khwājah
Bahā'al-Dīn Naqshband Bukhārī, the founder of the
Naqshbandiyyah Order.   Jāmī became a faithful disciple
and soon one of the most outstanding members of the
Naqshbandiyyah Order, also known as the order of the
Khwājagān (on Masters).   His works cannot be under-
stood save in the light of his having lived and practiced
Sufism.   Jāmī made two pilgrimages, one to the Holy
Cities of Mecca and Medina, and the other to Mashhad.
The rest of his life was spent quietly in Herat in following

---

[1] Plotinus himself was far from being a " harmless " philosopher in
the modern academic sage; rather he was a sage and metaphysician
definitely connected to a living esoteric tradition. But usually in
modern times his teachings have been used to obliterate the significance
and serious nature of the esoteric currents of the Islamic as well as Jewish
and Christian traditions.   See S. H. Nasr, introduction to the Arabic
version of Plotinus, *Enneads* ed. by S. J. Ashtiyānī, Tehran, 1978.

the spiritual life, study and writing. He even had a few spiritual disciples and also remained closely attached to the masters of the Naqshbandiyyah Order, especially to Khwājah Naṣīr al-Dīn Ahrār to whom Jāmī dedicated his *Tahfat al-ahrār* and who, after Sa‘d al-Dīn Kāshgarī, was the Naqshbandī master most close to Jāmī. It was the spiritual instructions of these masters which transformed the inner being of Jāmī and enabled him to compose, in simple and lucid language, masterpieces of Sufism of which the *Lawā'ih* is such a fine example. As Jāmī himself states in his *Nafahāt al-uns*, " The cause of blackening pages on Sufism was that when we began to delve into the works of these people [the Sufis], the comprehension of their purposes from the expressions they used was most difficult. We made a vow that if the gate were to be opened (and it became opened through spiritual wayfaring), the purposes of the people [the Sufis] would be expressed in such a way as to be easily comprehensible."[2]

Respected by king and beggar alike, Jāmī spent the rest of his fruitful life in Herat and died in the city of his birth in 898/1492. His tomb in that city is still a centre of pilgrimage where lovers of God gather to pay homage to one of the foremost gnostics of Islam who was at once a peerless poet, sage and scholar, one who lived and died in the sanctity of the Divine Presence.[3]

Jāmī is certainly one of the greatest poets of the Persian language and perhaps the most multi-faceted poetic

---

[2] *Nafahat al-uns*, ed. by M. Tawhīdīpur, Tehran, 1336 (A. H. solar), p. 17.

[3] Few Sufi poets have had their lives recorded as carefully as Jāmī. There are three authoritative accounts of his life by Radī al-Dīn ‘Abd al-Ghafur Lārī, ‘Alī ibn Ḥusayn Kāshifī and Mīr ‘Alīshīr Nawā'ī. For modern accounts of his life see E. C. Browne, *A Literary History of Persia*, vol. III, Cambridge, 1969, pp. 507–548; Cl. Huart and H. Massé, 'Djāmī', in the *New Encyclopaedia of Islam*; and W. Chittick, Persian and English introductions to his edition of Jāmī, *Naqd al-nusus fi sharh naqsh al-fusus*, Tehran–London, 1978.

genius of that tongue who was at the same time master of
lyrical, didactic, epic, moral and mystical poetry.   He was
at once related to Nizāmī and Amīr Khusraw, Saʿdī and
the line of Sanāʾī, ʿAttār, Rūmī and Ḥāfiz.   Certainly his
seven *mathnawīs*, known as the *Haft awrang*, are among
the undisputed masterpieces of Persian poetry and he has
even been entitled as the seal of Persian poets (*khātam
al-shuʿarāʾ*) although many fine poets came after him.   He
was, however, the last great Persian poet who was also an
outstanding gnostic and scholar.   Browne writes of him,
" [Jāmī] was one of the most remarkable geniuses whom
Persia ever produced, for he was at once a great poet, a
great scholar and a great mystic."[4]

The relation of Jāmī to various schools of Persian poetry
is the subject of literary history and cannot be dealt with
here.   What is of greater concern, as far as the *Lawāʾih* is
concerned, is Jāmī's role as the commentator of Ibn
ʿArabī and his school and his continuation of the tradition
of presenting the gnostic teachings of the school of Ibn
ʿArabī in Persian prose and poetry.   Muhyī al-Dīn ibn
ʿArabī was born in Murcia in Andalusia in 560/1165 and
died in Damascus in 638/1240.   He never came closer to
Persia than Baghdad,[5] but he was to have the profoundest
influence in nearly every aspect of the intellectual and

[4] Browne, *op. cit.*, p. 507.

[5] Concerning Ibn ʿArabī's life see S. H. Nasr, *Three Muslim Sages*,
Albany (N.Y.), 1976, chapter III, and M. Asin Palacios, *El Islam
Cristianizado, estudio del sufismo a travers de las obras de Abenarabi de
Murcia;* Madrid, 1939.   As for his doctrines and works see T. Burck-
hardt, *An Introduction to Sufi Doctrine*, trans. by D. M. Matheson, Lon-
don, 1976; T. Burckhardt (trs.), *La sagesse des prophètes*, Paris, 1955,
trans. from the French by A. Culme-Seymour, *Wisdom of the Prophets*,
London, 1975; T. Izutsu, *A Comparative Study of the Key Philosophical
Concepts of Sufism and Taoism—Ibn ʿArabi and Las Tsu*, Kyoto, 1967;
H. Corbin, *Creative Imagination in the Sufism of Ibn ʿArabi* trans.
R. Manheim, London, 1970.   Ibn ʿArabī, *Sufis of Andalusia* trans.
R. W. J. Austin, London, 1971; O. Yahya, *L'Histoire et la classification
des œuvres d'Ibn ʿArabi*, 2 vols., Damascus 1964.

spiritual life of Persia including not only Sufism itself but also philosophy and even theology.[6] This extensive influence, which caused over a hundred commentaries to be written by Persians upon the " seal (*khātam*) " of the works of Ibn 'Arabī, the *Fusūs al-hikam* (*Bezels of Wisdom*), is due to a large extent to the role played by Sadr al-Dīn Qunyawī in spreading the teachings of the master in the East.   Sadr al-Dīn who is one of the most neglected of the major figures of Sufism as far as contemporary scholarship is concerned,[7] himself trained several figures who wrote commentaries upon Ibn 'Arabī and composed works in both Arabic and Persian on this form of Sufism. Sadr al-Dīn's circle included not only such major literary figures as Fakhr al-Dīn 'Arāqī and Awhad al-Dīn Kirmānī but also such masters of gnosis as Mu'ayyid al-Dīn Jandī who wrote the first complete commentary upon the *Fusūs al-hikam*.

Jāmī was heir to both these " schools " or tendencies which emanated from the circle of Sadr al-Dīn Qunyawī, namely the school associated with the theoretical exposition of Sufi doctrine and the school of Persian literature, especially poetry, associated with gnosis (*al-ma'rifah* in Arabic and *'irfān* in Persian).   As far as the first school is concerned, Jandī was followed by Sa'd al-Dīn Farghānī, 'Abd al-Razzāq Kāshānī and Dā'ūd Qaysarī, all of whom wrote commentaries upon either Ibn 'Arabī or Ibn al-Fārid.   Jāmī was direct heir to these masters of gnosis and his own commentaries upon Ibn 'Arabī are based directly on the works of all of these luminaries of Sufism.[8]

---

[6] See " Seventy-century Sufism and the School of Ibn 'Arabī ", in Nasr, *Sufi Essays*, London 1972, pp. 97–103.

[7] A few articles and books have been devoted to him in Turkish and some of his writings have been printed in Arabic but not critically. G. Ruspoli and W. Chittick are now preparing works on him in French and English.

[8] On these figures and their influence upon Jāmī see the Persian introduction of W. Chittick to his edition of Jāmī's *Naqd al-nusūs*.

Jāmī was also direct heir to the Persian poetical tradition associated with the school of Ibn 'Arabī. Following
'Arāqī whose *Lamaʿāt* was composed after lessons given
by Sadr al-Dīn Qunyawī on the *Fusūs* and Awhad al-Dīn
who wrote beautiful quatrains based on the theme of the
" Transcendent Unity of Being " (*wahdat al-wujūd*),
several major poets completed the wedding between the
gnostic doctrines of Ibn 'Arabī and Persian Sufi literature,
especially poetry. These figures include Shaykh Mahmūd
Shabistārī whose *Gulshan-i rāz (Secret Rose Garden)* is perhaps the most perfect expression of pure *maʿrifah* in Persian poetry; Shams al-Dīn Maghribī whose *ghazals* are
nearly completely devoted to the theme of *wahdat al-
wujūd*; and Shāh Niʿmalallāh Walī, the founder of the
most widespread Sufi order in present-day Persia, whose
Dīwān and many prose treatises [9] reflect the teachings of
Ibn 'Arabī. Jāmī stands directly in the continuation of
this line although he is also profoundly related to the other
school of Sufism and Sufi poetry associated with Sanā'ī,
'Attār and Rūmī as well as Hāfiz.

Jāmī wrote the following works on the school of Ibn
'Arabī: [10]

1. *Naqd al-nusūs fī sharh naqsh al-fusūs (Selected Texts to
   Comment the " Imprint of the Fusūs ")*—the first major
   work of Jāmī on doctrinal Sufism and the basis of all
   his later works on the subject. In this opus which is
   half Arabic and half Persian, Jāmī quotes extensively
   from all the major commentators of Ibn 'Arabī preceding him, especially Qunyawī, Jandī and Farghānī.

2. *Sharh-i rubāʿiyyāt (Commentary upon the Quatrains (of*

---

[9] Both edited by J. Nourbakhsh, the present supreme master of the
order in Persia, the *Dīwan*, Tehran, 1354 (A.H. solar); and *Risālahā-yi
Hadrat-i Sayyid Nūr al-Dīn Shāh Niʿmatallāh Walī*, vol. I, Tehran,
1355 (A.H. solar)/2535; vol. II, Tehran, 1356 (A.H. solar)/2536.

[10] See Chittick, *op. cit.*, p. 21 on of the Persian introduction.

Jāmī)—A commentary by Jāmī upon some of his own quatrains to bring out their gnostic meaning.

3. *Lawā'ih* (*Gleaming Lights*)

The present work which is one of Jāmī's most important, and in which in a most lucid combination of Persian prose and poetry he summarises in a fresh manner the basic doctrines of Ibn 'Arabī and his school. It was written in 870/1465–66 and dedicated to the ruler Jahānshāh Qarahquyūnlū.

4. *Lawāmi'* (*Sparks of Inspiration*)

This is a commentary upon the *Khamriyyah* of Ibn al-Fārid with a long introduction on Ibn 'Arabī's doctrine of Being and Divine Love with the aid of which Ibn al-Fārid is interpreted. Some of the poems of Ibn al-Fārid are translated into exquisite Persian poetry.

5. *Sharh-i ba'dī az abyāt-i qasida-yi tā'iya-yi fāridiyyah* (*Commentary upon Some of the Verses of the Tā'iyyah of Ibn al-Fārid*

Seventy-five verses of the famous *Tā'iyyah* of Ibn al-Fārid, also known as the *Nazm al-sulūk* (*Poem of the Way*), are translated and commented upon in beautiful Persian.

6. *Ashi''at al-lama'āt* (*Rays from the Flashes* (*of 'Arāqī*))

A Persian commentary upon the *Lama'āt* of 'Arāqī, this work is one of the major prose treatises in Persian on doctrinal Sufism with an introduction containing a synopsis of the whole of Sufi doctrine and highly valued by later Sufis. The *Ashi''at al-lama'āt* has continued over the centuries as a basic text for the teaching of *'irfān* in Persia.

7. *Sharh fusūs al-hikam* (*Commentary upon the Fusūs al-hikam*)

This is the last of Jāmī's gnostic works commenting upon the *Fusūs* and like his first work on gnosis,

namely *Naqd al-nusūs*, based upon the well-known commentaries of Qunyawī, Jāndī, Farghānī, etc.[11]

The *Lawā'ih*, whose text and translation appears in the
pages which follow, is like a jewel in crown of the works of
Jāmī dealing with Sufism. Written in both prose and
poetry, it summarises in a remarkable fashion the teachings of the school Ibn 'Arabī concerning the Ultimate
Reality, its theophanies in the mirror of multiplicity and
the " Transcendent Unity of Being ". The prose exposi-
tions are punctuated by poems of great beauty which
reflect the beauty of the One and the importance of beauty
in Sufi doctrine.

What Jāmī exposes in the pages which follow is not the
fruit of simple speculation; rather it is the fruit of vision
made possible by spiritual discipline and the attainment
of sanctity. Gnosis is a *scientia sacra* and as Frithjof
Schuon, the outstanding master of the exposition of gnosis
in our times, has stated, " it is in the nature of the sacred
to demand of us all that we are ". To grasp fully the
doctrines stated in the *Lawā'ih* or any similar treatise of
Sufi doctrine, it is necessary to give oneself fully to the
Way which means to live according to tradition as revealed
by God through His prophets. At the same time, such
doctrine provides a *theoria* of the Truth whose actualisa-
tion and " tasting " (*dhawq*) can only come through
spiritual practice.[12] Such treatises enable those who possess the necessary intellectual qualifications to gain a

---

[11] See pp. 42 and 43 of Chittick's Persian introduction to the *Naqd al-nusūs*.

[12] See S. H. Nasr, *Science and Civilization in Islam*, New York, 1970,
chapter 13, where the importance of Sufi doctrine is clarified and the
basic doctrines of the " Transcendent Unity of Being " and " Universal
Man " (*al-insān al-kāmil*) summarised. On the comprehension of
doctrine based on the Absolute and its central importance in spiritual
realization, see F. Schuon, *Logic and Transcendence*, trans. P. Townsend,
New York, 1975; and his *Stations of Wisdom*, trans. G. E. H. Palmer,
London, 1961, pp. 13 ff.

vision from afar of the Truth.   As far as the presentation of the Truth in such authentic treatises of Sufi doctrine as the *Lawā'iḥ* is concerned, it is based on the inspiration of the author who has himself tasted the fruit of the Path. Its expression is therefore an art of the highest quality always combined with beauty which is inseparable from every authentic expression of the Truth.

The re-impression of this work after nearly three-quarters of a century is a sign of the continuous and in fact the ever-increasing interest in the West of the esoteric and metaphysical teachings of the East in general and of Sufism in particular and follows the general rise of devotion to the teachings of the school of Ibn 'Arabī.   Despite the many shortcomings of Whinfield's translation, it is our hope that the present work will be an aid to the discovery of the Truth which lies at the heart of the Islamic as well as all other integral traditions and whose rediscovery is the most urgent task before all who are concerned in more than a superficial fashion with the condition of man today.

Seyyed Hossein Nasr
Tehran
March 19, 1978 A.D.
9 Rabī' al-thānī 1398 A.H.

TRANSLATION OF THE LAWĀ'IH

" I DO not render praises unto Thee." [1] How is this, seeing that " all praise returns to Thee " ? [2] The threshold of Thy sanctity is too high for my praises. Thou art what Thine own praises declare Thee. O Lord, we are not able to tell Thy praises or set forth Thy glories. Whatsoever is manifested on the pages of the universe is praise reflected back to the threshold of Thy most glorious Majesty. What can faculty or tongue of mine declare worthy of Thy glory and honour ? Thou art such as Thou hast Thyself declared, and the pearls of Thy praise are what Thyself hast strung.

> In the vast largesse of Thy Majesty
> This whole world's but a drop from out the sea ;
> What power have we to celebrate Thy praise ?
> No praises save Thine own are meet for Thee !

Where the speaker of the words " I am the most eloquent [of the Arabs] " [3] lowered the flag of his eloquence, and found himself impotent to render Thee fitting praises, how shall a mere stammerer venture to open his mouth or a dullard deliver an apt discourse ? Nevertheless, in this case to excuse one's self on the ground of one's incapacity and deficiencies is itself the gravest of defects, and to put one's self on a level with that prince of the world and of the faith would be a serious breach of propriety.

[1] A saying of Muḥammad.
[2] Fluegel (Haji Khalfa, v, 344) translates, "Quomodo possim ?" Cf. Surah xvii, 46, " Neither is there aught which doth not celebrate Thy praise," and Psalm cxlv, 10.
[3] Referring to the saying " I am the most eloquent of those who pronounce the letter Zād (Dzād) ", the Arab shibboleth.

> What am I ? Can I count myself the peer
> Of the poor dog that's suffered to draw near ?
>   I may not join the caravan—enough
> If from afar the camel bells I hear.

O Lord, send down Thy blessing upon Muḥammad, the
standard-bearer of praise and possessor of " the glorious
station ",[1] and upon his family, and upon his companions
who through earnest endeavour have succeeded in attaining
the goal of their desire, and pour upon them all Thy
perfect peace !

SUPPLICATIONS [2]

O God, deliver us from preoccupation with worldly
vanities, and show us the nature of things " as they really
are ".[3] Remove from our eyes the veil of ignorance, and
show us things as they really are. Show not to us non-
existence as existent, nor cast the veil of non-existence
over the beauty of existence. Make this phenomenal
world the mirror [4] to reflect the manifestations of Thy
beauty, and not a veil to separate and repel us from Thee.
Cause these unreal phenomena of the universe to be for
us the sources of knowledge and insight, and not the
cause of ignorance and blindness. Our alienation and
severance from Thy beauty all proceed from ourselves.
Deliver us from ourselves, and accord to us intimate
knowledge of Thee.

> Make my heart pure, my soul from error free,
> Make tears and sighs my daily lot to be,
>   And lead me on Thy road away from self,
> That lost to self I may draw near to Thee !

[1] " It may be, O Muḥammad, that thy Lord will raise thee to
a glorious station " (Koran, xvii, 81), interpreted to mean his power of
intercession.

[2] The headings are all omitted in this manuscript, but spaces are left,
which were probably intended to be filled in with gold lettering.

[3] A prayer ascribed to Muḥammad. See *Gulshan i Rāz*, p. 21, n. 1

[4] The divine Real Being is reflected in " Not-being " (*'adm*) as in
a mirror, and gives it all the reality it possesses. See *Gulshan i Rāz*,
p. 14, l. 134. This idea comes from Plotinus, " the Shaikh of the
Greeks."

Set enmity between the world and me,
Make me averse from worldly company :
   From other objects turn away my heart,
So that it be engrossed with love to Thee.

How were it, Lord, if Thou shouldst set me free
From error's grasp and cause me truth to see ?
   Guebres by scores Thou makest Musulmans,
Why, then, not make a Musulman of me ?

My lust for this world and the next efface,
Grant me the crown of poverty, and grace
   To be partaker in Thy mysteries,
From paths that lead not towards Thee turn my face.

PREFACE

This is a treatise entitled *Lawā'iḥ*[1] ("Flashes of Light"),
explanatory of the intuitions and verities displayed on
the pages of the hearts and minds of men of insight
and divine knowledge, and of those who enjoy spiritual
raptures and ecstasies. It is written in suitable language
adorned with pleasing explanations. I trust that readers
will hold of no account the personality of the author of
this commentary, and will refrain from taking their seats
upon the carpet of cavilling and animadversion. For the
author plays only the part of interpreter in the following
discussions; his sole function is that of mouthpiece, and
nothing else.

Believe me, I am naught—yea, less than naught.
By naught and less than naught what can be taught ?
   I tell the mysteries of truth, but know
Naught save the telling to this task I brought.

For poverty to make no sign is best,
On love divine to hold one's peace is best ;
   For him who never felt ecstatic joys
To play a mere reporter's part is best.

---

[1] Haji Khalfa (v, 344) says Sayyid Kāseh Karrānī wrote a Persian
commentary upon it.

With men of light I sought these pearls to string,
The drift of mystics' sayings forth to bring ;
  Now let his trusty slaves this tribute bear
From foolish me to Hamadān's wise king.[1]

Flash I [2]

God has not made man with two hearts within him.[3]
The Incomparable Majesty who has conferred the boon of
existence upon thee has placed within thee but one heart,
to the end that with single heart thou mayest love Him
alone, and mayest turn thy back on all besides and devote
thyself to Him alone, and refrain from dividing thy heart
into a hundred portions, each portion devoted to a different
object.

    O votary of earthy idols' fane,
    Why let these veils of flesh enwrap thy brain ?
     'Tis folly to pursue a host of loves ;
    A single heart can but one love contain !

Flash II

Distraction or disunion (*Tafriqah*) consists in dividing
the heart by attaching it to divers objects. Union or
collectedness (*Jam'iyyat* [4]) consists in forsaking all else
and being wholly engrossed in the contemplation of the
One Unique Being. Those who fancy that collectedness
results from the collecting of worldly goods remain in
perpetual distraction, whilst those who are convinced that
amassing wealth is the cause of distraction renounce all
worldly goods.

---

[1] The person referred to is probably Shāh Mannchahr, Governor of
Hamadān, who paid much attention to Jāmī when he visited the town
in 877 A.H. See Lee's preface to the *Nafahāt*, p. 11. Note the pun on
" Hama Dān " (" All-knowing "). Amīr Sayyid 'Alī of Hamadān, a Ṣūfī
saint, is mentioned in the *Nafahāt*, p. 515, but as he died in 786 A.H. it
is not likely that Jāmī is speaking of him.

[2] " Lā'ihah." These headings, which are found in other manuscripts,
are omitted in this, as before remarked.

[3] Koran, xxxiii. 4.

[4] Also " tranquillity ", " congregation ", " totality ".

O thou whose heart is torn by lust for all,
Yet vainly strives to burst these bonds of all,
   This "all" begets distraction of the heart :
Give up thy heart to ONE and break with all.

While thou'rt distraught by hell-born vanity,
Thou'rt seen by men of union base to be ;
   By God, thou art a demon,[1] and no man,
Too ignorant thy devilry to see.

O pilgrim [2] on the "path", vain talk reject ;
All roads save that to Unity neglect ;
   Naught but distractedness proceeds from wealth:
Collect thine heart, not store of wealth collect.

O heart, thy high-prized learning of the schools,
Geometry and metaphysic rules—
   Yea, all but lore of God is devils' lore :
Fear God and leave this evil lore to fools.

Flash III

The " Truth ", most glorious and most exalted, is
omnipresent. He knows the outer and inner state of all
men in every condition. Oh, what a loss will be thine
if thou turnest thine eyes from His face to fix them on
other objects, and forsakest the way that is pleasing to
Him to follow other roads !

My Love stood by me at the dawn of day,
And said, " To grief you make my heart a prey;
   Whilst I am casting looks of love at you
Have you no shame to turn your eyes away ? "

All my life long I tread love's path of pain,
If peradventure " union " I may gain.
   Better to catch one moment's glimpse of Thee
Than earthly beauties' love through life retain.

Flash IV

Everything other than the " Truth " (may He be
glorified and exalted) is subject to decay and annihilation.

[1] *Nasnās* ; literally, a fabulous monster, a satyr.   [2] *Sālik*.

Its substance is a mental figment with no objective existence, and its form is a merely imaginary entity.

Yesterday this universe neither existed nor appeared to exist, while to-day it appears to exist, but has no real existence : it is a mere semblance, and to-morrow nothing thereof will be seen.   What does it profit thee to allow thyself to be guided by vain passions and desires ?   Why dost thou place reliance on these transitory objects that glitter with false lustre ?   Turn thy heart away from all of them, and firmly attach it to God.   Break loose from all these, and cleave closely to Him.   It is only He who always has been and always will continue to be.   The countenance of His eternity is never scarred by the thorn of contingency.

> The fleeting phantoms you admire to-day
> Will soon at Heaven's behest be swept away.
>   O give your heart to Him who never fails,
> Who's ever with you and will ever stay.
>
> When to fair idols' shrines I did repair,
> I vexed my heart with griefs encountered there ;
>   Now earthly beauty has lost all its charm,
> Eternal beauty is my only care.
>
> Things that abide not to eternity
> Expose thee to misfortune's battery ;
>   In *this* life, then, sever thyself from all
> From which thy death is bound to sever thee.
>
> Perchance with wealth and sons endowed thou art.
> Yet with all these erelong thou'lt have to part.
>   Thrice happy he who gives his heart to ONE,
> And sets affection on the men of heart.

Flash V

The Absolute Beauty is the Divine Majesty endued with [the attributes of] power and bounty.   Every beauty and perfection manifested in the theatre of the various grades of beings is a ray of His perfect beauty reflected therein.

It is from these rays that exalted souls have received their impress of beauty and their quality of perfection.[1] Whosoever is wise derives his wisdom from the Divine wisdom. Wherever intelligence is found it is the fruit of the Divine intelligence. In a word, all are attributes of Deity which have descended from the zenith of the Universal and Absolute to the nadir of the particular and relative. [They have descended] to the end that thou mayest direct thy course from the part towards the Whole, and from the relative deduce the Absolute, and not imagine the part to be distinct from the Whole, nor be so engrossed with what is merely relative as to cut thyself off from the Absolute.

> The Loved One's rose-parterre I went to see,
> That beauty's Torch[2] espied me, and, quoth He,
> "I am the tree; these flowers My offshoots are.
> Let not these offshoots hide from thee the tree."

> What profit rosy cheeks, forms full of grace,
> And ringlets clustering round a lovely face?
> When Beauty Absolute beams all around,
> Why linger finite beauties to embrace?

Flash VI

Man, in regard to his corporeal nature, stands at the lowest point of degradation; nevertheless, in regard to his spiritual nature, he is at the summit of nobility. He takes the impress of everything to which he directs his attention, and assumes the colour of everything to which he approaches. Wherefore philosophers say that when the reasonable soul adorns itself with exact and faithful impressions of realities, and appropriates to itself the true character of such realities, it becomes such as if it were itself altogether essential Being. In like manner

[1] Spenser in the "Hymn of Heavenly Love" expresses the same idea, which comes from Plato.

[2] Literally, "Torch of Tiráz," a town in Turkistán famed for its beautiful women.

the vulgar, by the force of their conjunction with these
material forms and extreme preoccupation with these
corporeal liens, come to be such that they cannot
distinguish themselves from these forms or perceive any
difference between the two.   Well says the Maulavī of
Rūm (may God sanctify his secret) in the *Masnavī*—

> O brother, thou art wholly thought,
> For the rest of thee is only bone and muscle :
> If thy thought be a rose, thou art a rose-bouquet ;
> If it be a thorn, thou art fuel for the fire.

Wherefore it behoves thee to strive and hide thy *self* from
thy sight,[1] and occupy thyself with Very Being, and
concern thyself with the " Truth ".   For the various
grades of created things are theatres of His revealed
beauty, and all things that exist are mirrors of his
perfections.

And in this course thou must persevere until He
mingles Himself with thy soul, and thine own individual
existence passes out of thy sight.   Then, if thou regardest
thyself, it is He whom thou art regarding ; if thou speakest
of thyself, it is He of whom thou art speaking.   The
relative has become the Absolute, and " I am the Truth "
is equivalent to " He is the Truth ".[2]

> If love of rose or bulbul fill thine heart,
> Thyself a rose or eager bulbul art.
>   Thou are a part ; the " Truth " is all in all.
> Dwell on the " Truth ", and cease to be a part.
>
> Of my soul's union with this fleshly frame,
> Of life and death Thou art the end and aim.
>   I pass away ; Thou only dost endure.
> When I say " me ", 'tis " Thee " I mean to name.[3]

[1] Variant, " hide thyself from the sight of the world."

[2] The saying of Manṣūr i Hallāj (or Ibn Hallāj), the Sūfī martyr.

[3] Compare the story of the Sūfī aspirant who was refused admittance
by his Pīr till he ceased to speak of " me " and called himself " thee "
(*Masnavī*, p. 47).

When will this mortal dress be torn away,
And Beauty Absolute His face display,
  Merging my soul in His resplendent light,
Blinding my heart with His o'erpowering ray ?

Flash VII

It is necessary for thee to habituate thyself to this intimate relation in such wise that at no time and in no circumstance thou mayest be without the sense of it, whether in coming or in going, in eating or sleeping, in speaking or listening. In short, thou must ever be on the alert both when resting and when working, not to waste thy time in insensibility [to this relation]—nay, more, thou must watch every breath, and take heed that it goeth not forth in negligence.

The years roll on ; Thou showest not Thy face,
Yet nothing from my breast Thy love can chase ;
  Thine image ever dwells before mine eyes,
And in my heart Thy love aye holds its place.

Flash VIII

In like manner, as it behoves thee to maintain the said relation continually, so it is of the first importance to develop the quality thereof by detaching thyself from mundane relations and by emancipating thyself from attention to contingent forms ; and this is possible only through hard striving and earnest endeavour to expel vain thoughts and imaginations from thy mind ; the more these thoughts are cast out and these suggestions checked, the stronger and closer this relation becomes. It is, then, necessary to use every endeavour to force these thoughts to encamp outside the enclosure of thy breast, and that the " Truth " most glorious may cast His beams into thy heart, and deliver thee from thyself, and save thee from the trouble of entertaining His rivals in thy heart. Then there will abide with thee neither consciousness of thyself,

nor even consciousness of such absence of consciousness [1]
—nay, there will abide nothing save the one God alone.

> From my brute nature,[2] Lord, deliver me,
> And from this life of evil set me free ;
>   Purge me of my own sense and ignorance,
> And make me lose my very self in Thee.

> When poor indeed and dead to self thou'lt need
> No visions, knowledge, certitude, or creed ;
>   When self has perished naught but God remains,
> For "Perfect poverty is God indeed".[3]

Flash IX

Self-annihilation consists in this, that through the
overpowering influence of the Very Being upon the inner
man there remains no consciousness of aught beside Him.
Annihilation of annihilation consists in this, that there
remains no consciousness even of that unconsciousness. It
is evident that annihilation of annihilation is involved in
[the very notion of] annihilation. For if he who has
attained annihilation should retain the least consciousness
of his annihilation, he would not be in the state of
annihilation, because the quality of annihilation and the
person possessing such quality are both things distinct
from the Very Being, the "Truth" most glorious.
Therefore, to be conscious of annihilation is incompatible
with annihilation.[4]

> While fondness for your "self" you still retain,
> You'll not reduce its bulk a single grain—
>   Yea, while you feel one hair's-breadth of yourself
> Claims to annihilation are but vain.

[1] See the passage from Ghazālī in Appendix III.

[2] *Dadī*, brutishness. Some manuscripts read *duwī*, disease, but this
does not suit the rhyme, which in verses with a burden (*radīf*) always
precedes it. Scan *dădĭyī*, dissolving long *ī* and lengthening the *izāfat*.

[3] Seemingly a Ḥadīth. Poverty, utter annihilation of self (*Gulshan
i Rāz*, l. 128 and note).

[4] So Ghazālī, quoted in Appendix III.

Flash X

Unification [1] consists in unifying the heart—that is to
say, in purifying it and expelling from it attachment
to all things other than the "Truth" most glorious,
including not only desire and will, but also knowledge and
intelligence.　In fact, one must quench desire of all things
hitherto desired, and cease to will what one has hitherto
willed, and also remove from the intellectual vision all
concepts and all cognitions, and turn away the mind
from all things whatsoever, so that there remains
no consciousness or cognition of aught save the
"Truth" most glorious.　Khwāja 'Abdullāh Anṣārī said :
"Unification is not merely believing Him to be One, but
in thyself being one with Him." [2]

> "Oneness" in pilgrims' phraseology
> Is from concern with "other" to be free ;
> 　Learn, then, the highest "station" of the birds, [3]
> If language of the birds be known to thee.

Flash XI

So long as a man remains imprisoned in the snare of
passions and lusts, it is hard for him to maintain this close
communion [with the "Truth"].　But from the moment
that sweet influence takes effect on him, expelling
from his mind the firebrand of vain imaginations
and suggestions, the pleasure he experiences therefrom
predominates over bodily pleasures and intellectual
enjoyments.　Then the painful sense of effort passes
away, and the joys of contemplation take possession of

---

[1] *Tauḥīd* is the *Henōsis* of Plotinus, the becoming one with the "One".

[2] This sentence occurs only in the British Museum copy, Add. 16819.
Khwāja 'Abdullāh Anṣārī of Herāt, who died 481 A.H., was named the
Shaikh of Islām, and is often quoted by Jāmī in the *Nafaḥāt*. See Haji
Khalfa, i, 235.

[3] Alluding to the "Discourse of the Birds and their Pilgrimage to the
Sīmurgh", by Farīd-ud-dīn 'Aṭṭār. "Other" the *Heterotēs* of Plotinus.

his mind; he banishes from his heart all alien distractions, and with the tongue of ecstasy murmurs this canticle—

> Like bulbul I'm inebriate with Thee,[1]
> My sorrows grow from memories of Thee,
>   Yet all earth's joys are dust beneath the feet
> Of those entrancing memories of Thee.

Flash XII

When the true aspirant perceives in himself the beginnings of this Divine attraction, which consists in experiencing pleasure whenever he thinks of the "Truth" most glorious, he ought to exert all his endeavours to develop and strengthen this experience, and simultaneously to banish whatever is incompatible therewith. He ought to know, for instance, that even though he should employ an eternity in cultivating this communion, that would count as nothing, and he would not have discharged his duty as he ought.

> On my soul's lute a chord was struck by Love,
> Transmuting all my being into love :
>   Ages would not discharge my bounden debt
> Of gratitude for one short hour of love.

Flash XIII

The essence of the "Truth" most glorious and most exalted is nothing but Being. His[2] Being is not subject to defect or diminution. He is untouched by change or variation, and is exempt from plurality and multiplicity; He transcends all manifestations, and is unknowable and invisible. Every "how" and "why" have made their

---

[1] So in the "Stabat Mater"—

"Fac me cruce inebriari."

[2] "The Truth" is also the One Real Agent, and therefore has the personal attribute of Will. Religion demands a personal object to worship. Hence Plato in the *Timæus* calls his Ideal Good "God", and the Latin version of the Nicene Creed substitutes *Dominus vivificans* for the neuter *To Kurion To Zōopoioun* of the original.

appearance through Him; but in Himself He transcends every "how" and "why". Everything is perceived by Him, while he is beyond perception. The outward eye is too dull to behold His beauty, and the eye of the heart is dimmed by the contemplation of His perfection.

> Thou, for whose love I've sacrificed existence,
> Art, yet art not, the sum of earth's existence ;
>   Earth lacks true Being, yet depends thereon—
> Thou art true Being : Thou art pure existence.

> The Loved One is quite colourless,[1] O heart ;
> Be not engrossed with colours, then, O heart :
>   All colours come from what is colourless,
> And "who can dye so well as God ",[2] O heart ?

Flash XIV

By the word " existence "[3] is sometimes meant simply the state of being or existing, which is a generic concept or an abstract idea. Taken in this sense, " existence " is an " idea of the second intention ",[4] which has no external object corresponding with it. It is one of the accidents of the " quidity "[5] [or real nature of the thing], which exists only in thought, as has been proved by the reasonings of scholastic theologians and philosophers. But sometimes " existence " signifies the Real Being, who is Self-existent, and on whom the existence of all other beings depends ; and in truth there is no real objective existence beside Him — all other beings are merely

---

[1] *Bīrangī*, absence of visible or knowable qualities.

[2] Koran, ii, 132.

[3] *Wajūd*, usually "necessary being" as opposed to " contingent ". Jāmī wrote a treatise on it, quoted in the *Dabistān*, ch. xii.

[4] *Ma'qūlāt i thānīyah*. In scholastic terminology terms of the second intention are those which express abstractions from concrete individual objects, e.g. genus, species, etc. Rabelais made fun of this term : " Utrum chimæra bombinans in vacuo comedere possit secundas intentiones ? "

[5] Quidity, what a thing is, a word derived by the Schoolmen from *māhīyat*. See Schmölders' *Documenta Philosophiæ Arabum*, p. 133.

accidents accessory to Him, as is attested by the intuitive
apprehension of the most famous Gnostics and "Men of
Certitude". The word ["existence"] is applicable to the
"Truth" most glorious in the latter sense only.

> Things that exist to men of narrow view
> Appear the accidents to substance due ;
>   To men of light substance is accident,
> Which the "True Being" ever doth renew.[1]

Flash XV

The attributes are distinct from the Real Being in
thought, but are identical with Him in fact and reality.
For instance, the Real Being is omniscient in respect of
His quality of knowledge; omnipotent in respect of His
power; absolute in respect of His will. Doubtless, just
as these attributes are distinct from each other in idea,
according to their respective meanings, so they are
distinct from the Real Being; but in fact and reality
they are identical with Him. In other words, there
are not in Him many existences, but only one sole
existence, and his various names and attributes are merely
His modes and aspects.

> Pure is Thy essence from deficiency,
> Expressed its "how" and "where" can never be ;
>   Thy attributes appear distinct, but are
> One with Thy essence in reality.

Flash XVI

The Real Being, quâ Being, is above all names and
attributes, and exempt from all conditions and relations.
The attribution to Him of these names only holds good in
respect of His aspect towards the world of phenomena.
In the first manifestation, wherein He revealed Himself,
of Himself, to Himself, were realized the attributes of
Knowledge, Light, Existence, and Presence. Knowledge

---

[1] "In Him we live, and move, and have our being" (Acts xvii, 28).

involved the power of knowing and that of being known ;
Light implied those of manifesting and of being manifest;
Existence and Presence entailed those of causing to exist
and of being existent, and those of beholding and of
being beheld. And thus the manifestation which is
a characteristic of Light is preceded by concealment;
and concealment, by its very nature, has the priority
over, and is antecedent to, manifestation ; hence the
concealed and the manifested are counted as first and
second.

And in like manner in the case of the second and third
manifestations, etc., as long as it pleases God to continue
them, these conditions and relations always go on
redoubling themselves. The more these are multiplied,
the more complete is His manifestation, or rather His
concealment. · Glory be to Him who hides Himself by the
manifestations of His light, and manifests Himself by
drawing a veil over His face. His concealment has
regard to His pure and absolute Being, while His
manifestation has regard to the exhibition of the world
of phenomena.

"O fairest rose,[1] with rosebud mouth," I sighed,
"Why, like coquettes, thy face for ever hide ? "
    He smiled, " Unlike the beauties of the earth,
    Even when veiled I still may be descried."

Thy face uncovered would be all too bright,
Without a veil none could endure the sight ;
    What eye is strong enough to gaze upon
The dazzling splendour of the fount of light ?

When the sun's banner blazes in the sky,
Its light gives pain by its intensity,
    But when 'tis tempered by a veil of cloud
That light is soft and pleasant to the eye.

---

[1] Cf. "Rosa mystica" in the Litany of the Virgin. Jalāl-ud-dīn
Rūmī apologizes for applying such terms to God (*Masnavī*, p. 34).

Flash XVII

The first Epiphany[1] is a pure unity and a simple potentiality, which contains all potentialities, including not only that of being unconditioned by modes and qualities, but also that of being conditioned thereby. Viewed as unconditioned by modes and qualities, including even the potentiality of being thus unconditioned, it is the stage termed "Unity"; and so possesses Concealment, Priority, and Existence from eternity. On the other hand, when viewed as conditioned by modes and qualities, it is the stage termed "Singleness", and in this aspect it is marked by Manifestation, Posteriority, and Duration to all eternity. Among these modes of the stage "Singleness", some are such that the qualification of the One Being by them has regard to the stage called the "Whole",[2] whether they imply the realization in the universe of things corresponding to the names "Creator" and "Sustainer", etc., or merely attributes, such as Life, Knowledge, and Will. This is the class of attributes which pertain to the Divinity and the Sovereignty. The forms under which the One Real Being is conceived, when clothed with these names and attributes, are the "divine substances".[3] The clothing of the outward aspect of Beings[4] with these forms does not necessitate multiplicity of beings. Other modes are such that the qualification of the One Real Being by them has relation

[4] *Ta'ayyun.* The first emanation is "Unity" with the "Truth" as being His image and mind (*Logos endiathetos*), but when evolved to view (*Logos prophorikos*), and as the channel of Being downwards, it is "Unity" with a difference, which is sought to be expressed by the term "Singleness" (*Wāḥidīyat* instead of *Aḥadīyat*).

[2] *Martaba i Jam'.* The second emanation, Universal Soul, which comprehends in itself all particular souls, rational, animal, and vegetive. This Aristotelian doctrine of the soul became a commonplace of the schools, and is referred to by Milton, Dryden, etc.

[3] Substance is *quod substat*, i.e. the reality underlying sensible phenomena. *Haqāiq i ilāhīya.*

[4] i.e. the first stage of His revelation.

to the various grades of "mundane existences",[1] as, for instance, Difference, Property,[2] and the phenomena which distinguish external objects from one another. The forms under which the One Real Being is conceived, when clothed with these modes, are "the mundane substances",[3] and the clothing of the outward aspect of Being with these forms *does* necessitate a multiplicity of beings. Among these mundane substances, some are such that when Being, considered in the stage of the "Unity of the Whole",[4] is interfused in them, and His effects and properties manifest themselves therein, these substances have the potentiality of being theatres exhibiting *all* the Divine names—save those peculiar to the Divine Essence— according to the varying strength of the manifestations, which may be powerful or feeble, irresistible or defeasible. These are the perfect individuals of the human race— to wit, prophets and saints. Others, again, are such that they have the potentiality of being theatres exhibiting only some of the Divine names, and not all of them, according to the aforesaid varying strength of the manifestation. These are the rest of the human race.

The Majesty of the One Real Being, viewed under the aspect of the "Unity of the Whole", which comprehends all His modes, both Divine and mundane,[5] is for ever immanent in all these substances, and manifesting Himself in them. These substances are the parts of the whole Unity, whether they exist in the world of spirits or in that of "ideas",[6] in the sensible and visible world, in the

---

[1] *Marātib i kauniya.*

[2] Difference, property, accident, genus, and species are the five heads under which Aristotle classed the general terms capable of being used as predicates.

[3] *Haqāiq i kauniya.*

[4] *Aḥadīyat i Jam'.* This is the second emanation (see Flash XXIV). It is usually called *nafs i kull*, or Universal Soul.

[5] i.e. plurality summed up in Unity.

[6] The plurality of "ideas" is the Platonic "intelligible" world of ideas or archetypes, apprehended only by Reason (*nous*) as opposed to the

world that now is, or in that which is to come. The
final Cause [1] of all this process is the realization or
manifestation of the perfection of the Divine names,
which is termed *jalā* and *istijlā*. *Jalā* signifies their
outward manifestation according to their various modes ;
and *istijlā* their display to the Deity Himself, according
to these same modes. *Jalā* is a visible and intelligible
manifestation or representation, just as the whole is
represented by its parts. Contrariwise, the perfection
of the Divine Essence is the manifestation of the One
Real Being to Himself, for Himself, without relation to
anything beside Himself. This is a secret and intelligible
manifestation.

Absolute self-sufficiency is a quality involved in Divine
Perfection. It signifies this, that in a general and
universal manner all the modes, states, and aspects of
the One Real Being with all their adherent properties
and qualities, in all their presentations, past, present, or
future, manifested in all grades of substances, Divine
and mundane, are present and realized in the secret
thought of that Divine Being, in such wise that the
sum of them all is contained in His Unity. From this
point of view He is independent of all other existences,
as it is said, "God most glorious can do without the
world" [2]—

> The robe of Love is independent, free
> From need to soil, with dust its purity ;
> When Actor and Spectator are the same
> What means this " we " and " thou "? There is
> no " we " [3]

"sensible" world of phenomena apprehended by the senses—*'ālam
i 'ilmī* as opposed to *'ālam i 'ainī*.

[1] In Aristotle's language the end (*telos*) of a thing is its "final cause",
i.e. the reason of its existence.

[2] Koran, xxix, 5.

[3] Cf. Omar Khayyām, Quatrain 475, and *Gulshan i Rāz*, p. 15, l. 143.
" He [God] is at once seer and thing seen."

All modes and attributes of Very Being
Are realized and present in that Being ;
   To see them He needs not contingent beings : [1]
'Tis the contingent needs the Very Being.

He needs not to see good and ill set out,
The One needs not to count its numbers out ; [2]
   The Truth can view all things within Himself ;
What need, then, to review them all without ?

Flash XVIII

When you abstract the appearances and characteristics
of the individual which constitute the various species
included in the genus "animal",[3] the individuals are
gathered up into their respective species. When, again,
you abstract the characteristics of each species, i.e. their
"differences" and "properties", all such species are
gathered up into the reality of the genus "animal ".
Again, when you abstract the characteristics of the genus
"animal" and those of all other genera included in the
higher genus "growing body", all such genera coalesce
under that genus "growing body ". So when you abstract
the characteristics of "growing body", and all other
genera included along with it under the higher genus
"body", all such genera are united in the reality of the
genus "body". Furthermore, when you abstract the
characteristics of "body" and those of all other genera
included therewith in the higher genus "substance", to

[1] Contingent being is opposed to necessary being. It is, so to speak,
unreal matter permeated with Real Being. "It thus is, and is not, and
partakes both of existence and of non-existence," as Jowett says.

[2] So Manṣur-i-Ḥallāj : " The numbers of Unity are only the counting
of Unity."

[3] The controversy of realism and nominalism raged among Moslems
as well as among European Schoolmen (see Schmölders, *Documenta*,
etc., p. 3). Jāmī was evidently a realist. He holds genus and similar
general terms to be actual realities (*ma'nī*), and not mere names. The
whole argument in this section rests on the assumption that these
genera are real entities.

wit, the "intelligences" and "souls", all such genera will be united in the reality of the higher genus "substance"; so when you abstract the characteristics distinctive of "substance" and "accident", these two genera are united into the [reality of the genus] "contingent". Finally, when you abstract the characteristic distinctions of "contingent" and "necessary", these two are united in the "Absolute Existence", which is the veritable Being, existing of Himself, and not through another being beyond Himself. "Necessity" is His external quality, and "Contingency" His internal quality—i.e. they are the "archetypal ideas" [1] generated by His self-revelation to Himself when assuming His "modes".

All these distinctions, whether called "difference" and "property" or "appearances" and "characteristics", are "Divine Modes", contained and involved in the "Unity of the One Real Being". First, these modes are represented under the form of the "archetypal ideas" in the stage called the "Divine Thought" (or knowledge);[2] in the next place, in the stage of the "sensible world", when clothed with the properties and attributes of external existence—which is the theatre of manifestation, a mirror reflecting the inner Divine Being—these modes assume the forms of external objects.

It follows, therefore, that in the external world there is only One Real Being, who, by clothing Himself with different modes and attributes, appears to be endued with multiplicity and plurality to those who are confined in the narrow prison of the "stages", and whose view is limited to visible properties and results.

---

[1] A'yān i thābitah, the "Ideas" of Plato's "Intelligible World", the archetypes or patterns of all things in the external and "sensible world". In the system of Plotinus these ideas are all contained in the first emanation, reason (nous). Jāmī expresses "intelligible world" by 'ālam i 'ilm, and "sensible world" by 'ālam i 'ain.

[2] Martaba i 'ilm, i.e. 'aql i kull, nous, or Logos, the first epiphany or emanation.

Creation's book I studied from my youth,
And every page examined, but in sooth
   I never found therein aught save the "Truth ",
And attributes that appertain to "Truth".

What mean Dimension, Body, Species,
In Mineral, Plant, Animal degrees ?
   The "Truth" is single, but His modes beget
All these imaginary entities.

Flash XIX

When one says that the multiplicity of things is
comprehended in the Unity of the One Real Being, this
does not mean that they are the parts contained in an
aggregate, or as objects contained in a receptacle, but
that they are as the qualities inherent in the object
qualified or as consequences flowing from their cause.
Take, for instance, the half, the third, the fourth, and
other fractions up to infinity, which are potentially[1]
contained in the integer, one, though not actually manifested until they are exposed to view by repeating the
various numbers and fractions.

It follows from this that when one says that the
"Truth" most glorious comprehends all beings, the
meaning is that He comprehends them as a cause
comprehends its consequences, not that He is a whole
containing them as His parts, or a vase containing things
within it. God is too exalted above everything which
is unworthy to touch the threshold of His holiness.[2]

These modes[3] are in the essence of the "Truth ",
Like qualities which qualify the "Truth";
   But part and whole, container and contained,
Exist not where God is, who is the "Truth ".

[1] Potentiality and actuality are two of Aristotle's forms of thought,
dunamis and *energeia* (*qūwat* and *fi'l*).

[2] God pervades everything, but everything is not God. Thus the
strict Monism of some previous statements is considerably toned down.

[3] *Shā'n.* The "Modalists" used the term "modes" to indicate
differences of form appearing in the One Substance (Harnack, *On Dogma*,
iii, 53), and thus to avoid ditheism.

Flash XX

The manifestation or concealment of the modes and facets—in other words, the circumstance that the outward aspect of Being does or does not clothe Himself with them —causes no change in the "substance" of such Being or in His essential attributes, but only a change in His connexions and relations, which. in fact, necessitates no change in His essence. For instance, if 'Amr gets up from the right of Zaid and goes and sits down on his left the relation of Zaid to 'Amr in respect to position will be changed, but his essence and his inherent qualities will remain unchanged.

Thus, the One Real Being underlying all outward existence does not become more perfect by clothing Himself with noble forms, nor does He degrade Himself by manifestation in inferior theatres. Although the light of the sun illuminates at once the clean and the unclean, yet it undergoes no modifications in the purity of its light; it acquires neither the scent of musk nor the colour of the rose, the reproach of the thorn nor the disgrace of the rugged rock.

> When the sun sheds his light for all to share,
> It shines on foul things equally with fair ;
> Fair things do not augment its radiance,
> Nor can foul things its purity impair

Flash XXI

The Absolute does not exist without the relative, and the relative is not formulated without the Absolute ; but the relative stands in need of the Absolute, while the Absolute has no need of the relative. Consequently, the necessary connexion of the two is mutual, but the need is on one side only, as in the case of the motion of a hand holding a key and that of the key thus held.

> O Thou whose sacred precincts none may see,
> Unseen Thou makest all things seen to be ;
> Thou and we are not separate, yet still
> Thou hast no need of us, but we of Thee.

Moreover, the Absolute requires a relative of some sort, not one particular relative, but any one that may be substituted for it. Now, seeing that there is no substitute for the Absolute, it is the Absolute alone who is the "Qibla" of the needs of all relatives.

> None by endeavour can behold Thy face,
> Or access gain without prevenient grace ; [1]
> For every man some substitute is found,
> Thou hast no peer, and none can take Thy place.

> Of accident or substance Thou hast naught,
> Without constraint of cause Thy grace is wrought ;
> Thou canst replace what's lost, but if Thou'rt lost,
> In vain a substitute for Thee is sought.

It is in regard to His essence that the Absolute has no need of the relative. In other respects the manifestation of the names of His Divinity and the realization of the relations of His Sovereignty are clearly impossible otherwise than by means of the relative.

> In me Thy beauty love and longing wrought :
> Did I not seek Thee how couldst Thou be sought ?
> My love is as a mirror in the which
> Thy beauty into evidence is brought.

Nay, what is more, it is the " Truth " who is Himself at once the lover and the beloved, the seeker and the sought. He is loved and sought in His character of the " One who is all " ; [2] and He is lover and seeker when viewed as the sum of all particulars and plurality.[3]

---

[1] *Faiz i azal.*
[2] *Maqām i Jam'i Aḥadīyat.* Note the change of phrase.
[3] *Martaba i tafṣīl wa kithrat.*

> O Lord, none but Thyself can fathom Thee,
> Yet every mosque and church doth harbour Thee ;
>   I know the seekers and what 'tis they seek—
> Seekers and sought are all comprised in Thee.

Flash XXII

The substance of each individual thing may be described
either as the epiphany of Very Being [1] in the "intelligible
world", according to the particular facet whereof such
thing is the monstrance, or as Very Being Himself made
manifest *immediately*,[2] in the same intelligible world and
according to the same facets. Consequently, each existing
thing is either an epiphany of Very Being with the colour
imparted to its exterior by the particular properties of its
substance, or the Very Being Himself immediately made
manifest with the same colouring.

The real substance of everything always abides, though
concealed in the inner depth of the Very Being, while its
sensible properties are manifest to outward sense.   For it
is impossible that the Divine " Ideas "[3] in the intelligible
world should be susceptible of evanescence, as that would
involve atheism.   [God is too exalted for such evanescence
to be ascribed to His " Ideas ".][4]

> We are the facets and the modes of Being,
> Evolved " Ideas "[5]—accidents of Being ;
>   We're hidden in the cloak of non-existence,
> But yet reflected in the glass of Being.[6]

[7][Consequently, everything is in reality and in fact
either Being made manifest or an accident of Being thus

---

[1] *Ta'ayyun i wajūd.*   [2] *Wajūd i muta'ayyin.*

[3] *Ṣuwar i 'ilmīya.*

[4] Blank left as usual for the Arabic sentence.

[5] i.e. the *'Ālam i 'ilm*, the intelligible world of the Divine " Ideas ".
Omit the second *dar* in line 2.

[6] Plotinus and the *Gulshan i Rāz* make not-being the mirror of Very
Being.   Jāmī here inverts the metaphor.

[7] The following passage omitted in this text.   It is probably a gloss
which has crept into some manuscripts.

manifested. The manifested accident is a quality of the manifested Being, and though in idea the quality is different from the thing qualified, yet in fact it is identical with it. Notwithstanding the difference in idea, the identity in fact justifies the attribution.[1]

> In neighbour, friend, companion, Him we see,
> In beggar's rags or robes of royalty ;
> In Union's cell or in Distraction's haunts,[2]
> There's none but He—by God, there's none but He.[3]]

Flash XXIII

Although the Very Being underlying all existence communicates Himself to all beings, both those in the intelligible and those in the sensible world, yet He does so in different degrees [some superior to others]. And in each of these degrees He has certain names, attributes, and modes, applicable to that particular degree and not to the others ; e.g. the names Divinity and Sovereignty [are not applicable] to the degrees called Subordination and the Creature-state. Consequently, to apply the names " Allah " and " the Merciful ", etc., to created beings is sheer infidelity and heresy. And, similarly, to apply the names suitable to grades of created things to the Deity is the height of misconception and delusion.

> O you who deem yourself infallible,
> In certitude a very oracle,[4]
> Each grade of beings has its proper name :
> Mark this, or you'll become an infidel.[5]

Flash XXIV

The Real Being is One alone, at once the true Existence and the Absolute. But He[6] possesses different degrees.

---

[1] *Ḥaml*, affirming a predicate of a subject.   [2] See Flash II.

[3] So *Gulshan i Rāz*, l. 883 : " See but One, say but One, know but One."

[4] *Ṣiddīq*, veracious, like Abu Bakr " as-Siddīq ".

[5] *Zindīq*.   [6] See n. 2, p. 12.

In the first degree He is unmanifested and unconditioned, and exempt from all limitation or relation. In this aspect He cannot be described by epithets or attributes, and is too holy to be designated by spoken or written words; neither does tradition furnish an expression for His Majesty, nor has reason the power to demonstrate the depth of His perfection. The greatest philosophers are baffled by the impossibility of attaining to knowledge of Him ; His first characteristic is the lack of all characteristics, and the last result of the attempt to know him is stupefaction.[1]

> To you convictions and presumptions wrought
> By evidence intuitive are naught ;
> How can one prove your own reality
> To such as you who count all proofs as naught ?
>
> However great our heavenly knowledge be,
> It cannot penetrate Thy sanctuary ;
> Saints blest with visions and with light divine
> Reach no conceptions adequate to Thee.
>
> Our love,[2] the special grace of souls devout,
> To reason seems a thing past finding out ;
> Oh, may it bring the dawn of certitude,
> And put to flight the darksome hours of doubt !

The second degree is the self-display of Very Being in an epiphany containing in itself all the active, necessary, and divine manifestations, as well as all the passive, contingent, and mundane manifestations. This degree is named the " First Emanation ",[3] because it is the first of all the manifestations of the Very Being ; and above it there is no other degree than that of the "Unmanifested ".

---

[1] *Ḥairānī*. In the *Manṭiq uṭ-Ṭair*, *Hairat* is the last valley in the Ṣūfī pilgrim's progress. To know God he must rise to ecstasy.

[2] Rūmī describes love as spiritual clairvoyance. See *Masnavī*, Introduction, p. xxviii.

[3] *Ta'ayyun i awwal*, usually called *'aql i kull*, universal reason, i.e. *nous* or *Logos*, as by Jāmī himself in *Salāman wa Absal*. " The first thing created was reason " (Ḥadith).

The third degree is named the " Unity of the Whole Aggregate ",[1] which contains in itself all the active and efficient manifestations. It is named the degree of " Divinity ".[2]

The fourth degree is the manifestation. in detail of the degree named Divinity; it is the degree of the names and the theatres wherein they are manifested. These two last-named degrees refer to the outward aspect of Being wherein " necessity " [3] is a universal condition.

The fifth degree is the " Unity of the Whole Aggregate ", which includes all the passive manifestations whose characteristic is the potentiality of receiving impressions, i.e. passivity. It is the degree of mundane existence and contingency.[4]

The sixth degree is the manifestation in detail of the preceding degree ; it is the degree of the sensible world.[5] These two last degrees refer to the exterior of the intelligible world,[6] wherein contingence is one of the invariable qualities. It consists of the revelation of the Divine Mind to Himself under the forms of the substances of the contingent.

Consequently, in reality there is but One Sole Being, who is interfused in all these degrees and hierarchies which are only the details of the Unity (" Singleness ").[7] " Very Being " in these degrees is identical with them, just as these degrees when they were in the Very Being were identical therewith. [" God was, and there was not anything with Him."] [8]

---

[1] *Aḥadiyat i Jam'*, usually called *nafs i kull*, universal soul, *pneuma*.

[2] *Ilāhīyat.* See De Sacy's note in *Notices et Extraits des Manuscrits*, x, 77.

[3] *Wajūb.* It belongs to the sphere of " Necessary Being ".

[4] *Martaba i kaunīya i imkānīya.*   [5] *'Ālam.*

[6] The object of this distinction is to keep God from contact with matter. Contingency is not found in the *immediate* reflections of Being, but only in the reflections from the intelligible world of Divine Ideas.

[7] *Wāhidīyat.* See n. 1, p. 16.

[8] A saying attributed to Muḥammad. A blank is left for it in this manuscript.

The " Truth " appears in all ; wouldst thou divine
How with Himself He doth all things combine ?
   See the wine-froth : the wine in froth is froth,
Yet the froth on the wine is very wine.

'Tis the bright radiance of Eternity
That lights Not-being, as we men may see ;
   Deem not the world is severed from the " Truth ":
In the world He's the world, in Him 'tis He.

Flash XXV

The " Truth of truths ", which is the essential, most
exalted Divine Being, is the Reality in all things. He is
One in Himself, and " unique " in such wise that plurality
cannot enter into Him ; but by His multiple revelations
and numerous phenomenal displays He is sometimes
presented under the form of substantial independent
entities,[1] and at other times under the form of accidental
and dependent entities.[2] Consequently, the One Essential
Being appears as multiple by reason of the numerous
qualities of these substances and accidents, although in
point of fact He is " One ", and is in no wise susceptible
of numbers or plurality.

Rase the words " this " and " that "; duality
Denotes estrangement and repugnancy ;
   In all this fair and faultless universe
Naught but one Substance and one Essence see.[3]

This unique Substance, viewed as absolute and void of
all phenomena, all limitations, and all multiplicity, is the
" Truth ". On the other hand, viewed in His aspect of
multiplicity and plurality, under which He displays
Himself when clothed with phenomena, He is the whole
created universe. Therefore the universe is the outward
visible expression of the " Truth ", and the " Truth " is

---

[1] *Haqāiq i Jauharīya i maṭbū‘a.*
[2] *Haqāiq i ‘arazīya i ṭābi‘a.*
[3] See n. 3, p. 25.

the inner unseen reality of the universe. The universe
before it was evolved to outward view was identical
with the " Truth " ; and the " Truth " after this evolution
is identical with the universe. Nay, more, in reality
there is but One Real Being ; His concealment [in the
Divine Mind] and His manifestation [in the sensible
world], His priority and His posteriority [in point of time],
are all merely His relations and His aspects. " It is
He who is the first and the last, the exterior and the
interior." [1]

> In the fair idols, goal of ardent youth,
> And in all cynosures [2] lies hid the " Truth ";
> What, seen as relative, appears the world,
> Viewed in its essence is the very " Truth ".

> When in His partial modes Truth shone out plain,
> Straightway appeared this world of loss and gain ;
> Were it and all who dwell there gathered back
> Into the Whole, the " Truth " would still remain.[3]

Flash XXVI

The Shaikh [4] (may God be well pleased with him)
says in the Faṣṣ i Shu'aibī, that the universe consists of
accidents all pertaining to a single substance, which is
the Reality underlying all existences. This universe is
changed and renewed unceasingly at every moment and
at every breath. Every instant one universe is annihilated
and another resembling it takes its place, though the
majority of men do not perceive this, as God most glorious
has said . [" But they are in doubt regarding the new
creation." [5]]

---

[1] Koran, lvii, 3. Cf Rev. i, 8, " I am Alpha and Omega."

[2] Literally, " horizons," i.e. objects of aspiration.

[3] i.e. the grade of plurality in Unity, or Universal Soul.

[4] Muhiyi-ud-dīn Muhammad Andalūsī, commonly called Ibn 'Arabi,
died 638 A.H. Wrote the Faṣūṣ-ul Hikam (Haji Khalfa, iv, 424). Each
section is named after some patriarch, e.g. Shu'aib (Jethro).

[5] Koran, l, 14. See Gulshan i Rāz, l. 670. Text omitted in this
manuscript.

Among Rationalists [1] no one has perceived this truth with the exception of the Asharians,[2] who recognize it in certain departments of the universe, to wit, "accidents," as when they say that accidents exist not for two moments together; and also with the exception of the Idealists,[3] called also Sophists, who recognize it in all parts of the universe, whether substances or accidents. But both these sects are in error in one part of their theory. The Asharians are wrong in asserting the existence of numerous substances—other than the One Real Being underlying all existence—on which substances, they say, depend the accidents which continually change and are renewed. They have not grasped the fact that the universe, together with all its parts, is nothing but a number of accidents, ever changing and being renewed at every breath, and linked together in a single substance, and at each instant disappearing and being replaced by a similar set. In consequence of this rapid succession, the spectator is deceived into the belief that the universe is a permanent existence. The Asharians themselves declare this when expounding the succession of accidents in their substances as involving continuous substitution of accidents, in such wise that the substances are never left wholly void of accidents similar to those which have preceded them. In consequence of this the spectator is misled into thinking that the universe is something constant and unique.[4]

[1] *Ahl-i nazr*, as opposed to *ahl-i shahūd*, men of spiritual intuition.

[2] The followers of Abū-l Ḥasan al Ashārī, died about 330 A H. (Ibn Khallikan, ii, 227).

The *Ḥasbāniya*.

[4] This is the Heracleitean doctrine that all phenomena are in constant flux, issuing from the "Fiery Breath" (*Pneuma*) and remerged in it every moment. Jalāl-ud-dīn quotes the saying of "Arqlitus" that "Contraries are congruous", the first suggestion of the Hegelian doctrine that contraries always involve a higher unity which embraces both. See Lumsden, *Persian Grammar*, ii, 323.

The ocean does not shrink or vaster grow,
Though the waves ever ebb and ever flow ;
   The being of the world's a wave, it lasts
One moment, and the next it has to go.

In the world, men of insight may discern
A stream whose currents swirl and surge and churn,
   And from the force that works within the stream
The hidden working of the " Truth " may learn.

As regards the Sophists, though they are right in asserting the ideality of the whole universe, they are wrong in failing to recognize the Real Being underlying it, who clothes Himself with the forms and accidents of the sensible universe and appears to us under the guise of phenomena and multiplicity ; likewise in denying any manifestation of Real Being in the grades of visible things under the guise of these forms and accidents, whereas in truth these accidents and forms are only manifested to outward view by the operation of that underlying Real Being.

   Philosophers devoid of reason find
   This world a mere idea of the mind ,
      'Tis an idea—but they fail to see
   The great Idealist who looms behind.

But the men gifted with spiritual intuition see that the Majesty of the " Truth ", most glorious and most exalted, reveals Himself at every breath in a fresh revelation,[1] and that He never repeats the same revelation ; that is to say, He never reveals Himself during two consecutive moments under the guise of the same phenomena and modes, but every moment presents fresh phenomena and modes.

   The forms which clothe existence only stay
   One moment, in the next they pass away ;
      This subtle point is proven by the text,
   " Its fashion altereth from day to day." [2]

[1] See *Masnavi*, p. 24.   [2] Koran, lv, 29.

The root of this mystery lies in the fact that the Majesty of the " Truth " most glorious possesses " names " opposed [1] to one another, some being beautiful and some terrible ; and these names are all in continuous operation,[2] and no cessation of such operation is possible for any of them. Thus, when one of the contingent substances, through the concurrence of the requisite conditions, and the absence of opposing conditions, becomes capable of receiving the Very Being, the mercy of the Merciful takes possession of it, and the Very Being is infused [3] into it; and the Very Being thus externalized,[4] through being clothed with the effects and properties of such substances, presents Himself under the form of a particular phenomenon, and reveals Himself under the guise of this phenomenon. Afterwards, by the operation of the terrible Omnipotence which requires the annihilation of all phenomena and all semblance of multiplicity, this same substance is stripped of these phenomena. At the very moment that it is thus stripped this same substance is reclothed with another particular phenomenon, resembling the preceding one, through the operation of the mercy of the Merciful One. The next moment this latter phenomenon is annihilated by operation of the terrible Omnipotence, and another phenomenon is formed by the mercy of the Merciful One ; and so on for as long as God wills. Thus, it never happens that the Very Being is revealed for two successive

[1] *Lutf* and *Qahr*, or *Jamāl* and *Jalāl*, the opposite Divine attributes of mercy and vengeance, beauty and terror. The Divine economy is sometimes represented as effected by the eternal struggle between these two opposite phases of Deity, as manifested in Adam and Iblīs, Abraham and Nimrod, Moses and Pharaoh, etc. (see *Masnavī*, p. 301), a daring Monist hypothesis, which, needless to say, is not pursued into its consequences.

[2] These "names", like the Stoic *logoi*, are sometimes spoken of as ideas, sometimes as forces or energies.

[3] *Ifāzat*, production by emanation. See *Notices et Extraits des Manuscrits*, x, 66.

[4] *Sein* evolved into *dasein*.

moments under the guise of the same phenomenon. At every moment one universe is annihilated and another similar to it takes its place. But he who is blinded by these veils, to wit, the constant succession of similar phenomena and like conditions, believes that the universe constantly endures in one and the same state, and never varies from time to time.

> The glorious God, whose bounty, mercy, grace,
> And loving-kindness all the world embrace,
>   At every moment brings a world to naught,
> And fashions such another in its place.

> All gifts soever unto God are due,
> Yet special gifts from special "names" ensue ;
>   At every breath one "name" annihilates,
> And one creates all outward things anew.

The proof that the universe is nothing more than a combination of accidents united in a single essence, i.e. the "Truth" or Very Being, lies in the fact that when one comes to define the nature of existing things these definitions include nothing beyond "accidents". For example, when one defines man as a "rational animal"; and animal as a "growing and sentient body, possessed of the faculty of voluntary movement"; and body as a "substance possessing three dimensions"; and substance as an "entity which exists *per sé* and is not inherent in any other subject"; and entity as "an essence possessed of reality and necessary being"—all the terms used in these definitions come under the category of "accidents", except this vague essence which is discerned behind these terms. For "rational" signifies an essence endued with reason; "that which is growing" signifies an essence endued with the faculty of growth ; and so on. This vague essence is, in fact, the "Truth", the Very Being, who is self-existent, and who causes all these accidents to exist. And when the philosophers allege that these terms do not express the differences themselves, but only the invariable marks of these differences whereby we express them, because it is impossible to express the true differences otherwise than by these invariable marks or others more recondite still, this assumption is inadmissible and undeserving of serious attention. And even if we admit it as a hypothesis, we affirm that whatever is essential in relation to special substances is accidental in relation to the Very Truth; for though this alleged essential quality is part of the essence of a particular substance, it is extraneous to the Very Truth upon whom it is dependent. And to say that there is any substantial entity other than the One Essential Being is the height of error, especially when the spiritual intuition of the men of truth, which is borrowed from the lamp of prophecy, attests the contrary,[1] and when their opponents cannot cite any proofs in favour of their own view. ["God saith what is true, and directeth man in the right path."[2]]

> Truth is not proved by terms and demonstrations,
> Nor seen when hidden by concrete relations;[3]
> The "Canon" is no "Cure" for ignorance,
> Nor can "Deliv'rance" come from "Indications".[4]

> If at each "Stage" thy course diverted be
> To different "Goals", true goal thou'lt never see;
> And till the veil is lifted from thine eyes
> The sun of Truth will never "Rise" for thee.[5]

[1] Cf. 1 Cor. ii, 15, "He that is spiritual judgeth all things, yet he himself is judged of no man." Or, as Hegelians would put it, the deliverances of intuitive reason are not to be tried by the canons of the discursive reason (*verstand*).

[2] Koran, xxxiii, 4. A blank is again left for the text in this manuscript.

[3] *Quyūd.*

[4] Alluding to four famous works of Ibn Sīnā (Avicena), *Shifā*, *Qānūn*, *Nijāt*, and *Ishārāt*.

[5] Alluding to *Mawāqif*, a theological work by Al Ijī; *Maqāṣid*, by Al Taftāzānī; and *Maṭāli'*, a work on logic by Al Ormawī. See Otto Loth, *Catalogue of India Office Arabic Manuscripts*, pp. 114, 460, and 143.

> Strive to cast off the veil, not to augment
> Book-lore : no books will further thy intent.
>   The germ of love to God grows not in books ;
> Shut up thy books, turn to God and repent.

The completest mask and the densest veils of the beauty of the One Real Being are produced by the manifold limitations which are found in the outward aspect of Being and which result from His being clothed with the properties and effects of the archetypes indwelling in the Divine Knowledge,[1] which is the inner side of Being. To those blinded by these veils it seems that the archetypes exist in these outward sensible objects, whereas in point of fact these outward objects never attain a particle[2] of those real archetypes, but are and will always continue in their original not-being. What exists and is manifested is the "Truth", but this is only in regard to His being clothed with the properties and effects of the archetypes, and not in regard to His condition when bare of all these properties; for in this latter case inwardness and conceal-ment are amongst His inherent qualities. Consequently, in reality the Very Being never ceases to abide in His Essential Unity, wherein He was from all eternity and wherein He will endure to all eternity. But to the vulgar, who are blinded by these veils, the Very Being seems to be relative and phenomenal, and wearing the form of the multiplicity of these properties and effects, and He seems manifold to such persons.

> Being's a sea in constant billows rolled,[3]
> 'Tis but these billows that we men behold ;
>   Sped from within, they rest upon the sea,
> And like a veil its actual form enfold.

---

[1] *A'yān i thābitah dar ḥazrat i 'ilm*, the Ideas or archetypes in Plato's "Intelligible World" (see *Notices et Extraits des Manuscrits*, x, 65). *'Ain* has the double meaning of " eye " and " essence ", and its derivatives *A'yān* and *Ta'ayyun* are used to denote the reflections of the One Being ; in other words, His emanations which constitute the existences or substances in the world of visible and sensible phenomena (*'Ālam i 'Ain*).

[2] Literally, " smell."   [3] See *Masnavi*, p. 42.

> Being's the essence of the Lord of all,
> All things exist in Him and He in all ;
>   This is the meaning of the Gnostic phrase,
> " All things are comprehended in the All."

[1] [When one thing is manifested in another, the thing manifested is different from the thing which is the theatre of the manifestation—i.e. the thing manifested is one thing and its theatre another. Moreover, that which is manifested in the theatre is the image or form of the thing manifested, not its reality or essence. But the case of the Very Being, the Absolute, is an exception, all whose manifestations are identical with the theatres wherein they are manifested, and in all such theatres He is manifested in His own essence.

> They say, How strange ! This peerless beauty's face
> Within the mirror's heart now holds a place ;[2]
>   The marvel's not the face, the marvel is
> That it should be at once mirror and face.

> All mirrors in the universe I ween
> Display Thy image with its radiant sheen—
>   Nay, in them all, so vast Thy effluent grace,
> 'Tis Thyself, not Thine image, that is seen.

The " Truth ", the Very Being, along with all His modes His attributes, connexions, and relations, which constitute the real existence of all beings, is immanent in the real existence of each being. Hence it has been said, " The All exists in all things." The author of the *Gulshan i Rāz* says :

> " If you cleave the heart of one drop of water
> There will issue from it a hundred pure oceans."[3]]

Every power and every act manifested as proceeding from the theatres of manifestation proceed in reality from

---

[1] The following passage in brackets is omitted in this manuscript.

[2] In the *Gulshan i Rāz*, l. 134, Very Being is said to be reflected in the mirror of not-being.

[3] Verse 146.

the "Truth" manifested in these theatres, and not from
the theatres themselves. The Shaikh (may God be well
pleased with him) says in the *Hikmat i 'Aliyya* :[1] "Outward existence (*'ain*) can perform no act of itself; its acts
are those of its Lord immanent in it; hence this outward
existence is passive, and action cannot be attributed to it."
Consequently, power and action are ascribed to the
creature (*'abd*) because of the manifestation of the
"Truth" under the form of the creature, and not because
such action is really effected by the creature himself.
[Read the text: "God hath created thee, both thee and
the works of thy hands"[2]], and recognize the fact that
thy existence, thy power, and thine actions come from the
Majesty of Him who has no equal.[3]

> Both power and being are denied to us,
> The lack of both is what's ordained for us ;
>   But since 'tis He who lives within our forms,
> Both power and action are ascribed to us.

> Your "self" is non-existent, knowing one !
> Deem not your actions by yourself are done ;
>   Make no wry faces at this wholesome truth—
> "Build the wall ere the fresco is begun."

> Why vaunt thy "self" before those jealous eyes ?[4]
> Why seek to deal in this false merchandise ?
>   Why feign to be existent of thyself ?
> Down with these vain conceits and foolish lies !

Flash XXVII

Since the qualities, states, and actions manifested in the
theatres are in reality to be ascribed to the Very Being
manifested in those theatres, it follows that if a certain

[1] The Shaikh Muhiyi-ud-dīn Ibn al 'Arabī. The "Hikmat i 'Aliyya"
is the first section of his *Faṣūṣ ul Hikam.*

[2] Koran, xxxvii, 94. A blank left for the text.

[3] The Ṣūfīs call God the "One Real Agent"—*Fā'il i Haqīqī.*
Determinism is a necessary corollary of Monism.

[4] Cf. the Hadith "God is more jealous than Sa'd" (*Masnavi*, p. 29,
note). Self-assertion is presumption towards God.

evil or imperfection is found in any of them, it may
possibly be caused by the non-existence of something else ;
for Being, *quâ* Being, is pure good ; and whenever it seems
to us that something existent contains evil, *that* is owing
to the lack of something else which ought to exist, and
not to the really existing Being, *quâ* Being.[1]

> All good and all perfection that you see
> Are of the " Truth ", which from all stain is free;
>   Evil and pain result from some defect,
> Some lack of normal receptivity.

Philosophers have alleged that the proposition " Very
Being is pure good " is a necessary (self-evident) one.[2]
By way of illustration, they have given some examples.
Thus, they say cold, which spoils the fruit and is an evil
in relation to the fruit, is not an evil [absolutely], because
it is one of the qualities [of Being], and in this respect
one of His perfections ; but [it is evil] because it prevents
the fruit attaining the perfection proper to it.   Thus, too,
killing, which is an evil, is not an evil by reason of the
murderer's power of killing, nor by reason of the power
of the instrument to cut, nor of the liability of the body
of the person killed to be cut ; but [it is an evil] because
it deprives a person of life, which is the mere negation
[of something positive] ;[3] and so on.

> Wherever Being's ambit doth extend,
> Good and nought else but good is found, O friend;
>   All evil comes from " not-being ", to wit,
> From " other ", and on " other " must depend.[4]

[1] " Being is good in whatever it be. If a thing contains evil, *that*
proceeds from ' other ' " (*Gulshan i Râz*, l. 871). Augustine, like Jāmī,
makes evil merely a deficiency of good. See *Confessions*, book vii, ch. xii.

[2] *Zarūrat.*   Necessary truths are those of which the contrary is
inconceivable.   Of course, in Jāmī's time necessity of thought was
supposed to involve necessity of the object of thought.

[3] Just so Spinoza boldly argues that the evil element in Nero's
matricide was not positive but only negative, not reality (*essentia*) but
defect of reality, viz. want of natural affection and pity.   Froude, *Short
Studies*, i, 364.

[4] *Gulshan i Râz*, l. 871.

Flash XXVIII

Shaikh Ṣadr-ud-dīn Qūniavī (may God sanctify his secret) says in the book *Nuṣūṣ*[1]: " Knowledge is one of the qualities pertaining to Being; that is to say, that every existing substance is endued with knowledge ; and the difference in the degrees of knowledge results from the differences of these substances in their reception, whether perfect or imperfect, of Being. Thus a substance capable of receiving Being in a most complete and perfect way is capable of receiving knowledge in the same way; and that which is only capable of receiving Being imperfectly is endued with knowledge in the same degree. This difference originates in the stronger or weaker influence of ' necessity '[2] or ' contingency ' over each substance. In every substance in which the influence of ' necessity ' is the stronger, Being and knowledge are most perfect ; in the remainder, in which the influence of ' contingency ' is more prevalent, Being and knowledge are more imperfect."

It would seem that what the Shaikh states as to knowledge specially being a quality appertaining to Being is meant to convey one example only, because all the other perfections which are likewise qualities pertaining to Being, such as life, power, will, etc., are in the same position as knowledge.

Certain other [Ṣūfīs] have said : " No single existent thing is without the quality of knowledge "; but knowledge is of two kinds, one ordinarily called knowledge and the other not so called. Both kinds, according to the men of truth, belong to the category of knowledge, because they recognize the immanence of the essential knowledge of the " Truth " most glorious and most exalted in all

---

[1] *An-Nuṣūṣ fī taḥqīq i ṭaur il makhṣūṣ*, by the celebrated Ṣūfī Shaikh Ṣadr-ud-dīn Muḥammad bin Isḥāq al Qūniavī, died 672 A.H. See Haji Khalfa, vi, 349.

[2] The more " necessary being " a thing has, the less it has of " contingent being ", i.e. less intermixture with not-being. See n. 1, p. 19.

things whatsoever. It is in the second class that we must place " water ", for example, which is not ordinarily considered as possessed of knowledge. But we see that it distinguishes between up and down hill ; it avoids the rise and runs downwards ; again, it sinks into porous bodies, whilst it only wets the surface of dense bodies and passes over them, etc. Therefore, it is by virtue of the quality of knowledge that it runs, according to the capacity of one object to admit it, and the absence of opposing properties in such objects. But, in this degree, knowledge is manifested only under the form of nature.[1] In this manner knowledge is immanent in all other existing things ; or, rather, all perfections pertaining to Being are immanent in all things without exception.

> Being, with all its latent qualities,
> Doth permeate all mundane entities,
>   Which, when they can receive them, show them forth
> In the degrees of their capacities.

Flash XXIX

Just as the " Truth ", the Very Being, in virtue of His absolute purity, is immanent in the substances of all beings in such wise as to be essentially identical with these substances, as these substances are, when in Him, identical with Him ; in like manner His perfect qualities are entirely and absolutely immanent in all qualities of the substances in such wise as to be identical with their qualities, even as their qualities when in those perfect qualities were identical therewith. For example, the quality of knowledge, in the knowledge of the knower of particulars,[2] is identical with this knowledge of particulars, and in the knowledge of him who knows universals[2] is identical with this knowledge of universals ; in active and

---

[1] i.e. in unconscious objects. Thus Aristotle says plants seek their own perfection unconsciously, while man does it consciously.

[2] *Juzviyāt* and *kulliyāt*.

passive[1] knowledge it is identical with such knowledge ;
in ecstatic and mystic[2] knowledge it is identical with that
kind of knowledge—similarly down to the knowledge of
those beings not ordinarily classed as having knowledge,
wherein it is identical with such knowledge in a manner
suitable to the character of such beings, and so on for
the other Divine attributes and qualities.[3]

> Thy essence permeates all entities,
> As do Thy attributes all qualities ;
>> In Thee they're absolute, but when displayed
>> They're only seen in relative degrees.[4]

[[5]The reality of existence is the essence[6] of the "Truth"
most glorious and most exalted ; the modes, relations, and
aspects of existence are His attributes ;[7] His manner of
manifesting Himself in the vesture of these relations and
aspects is His action and His impress ;[8] the phenomena
manifested and proceeding from this self-revelation are
the products of His impress.[9]

> Th' essential modes in earth and heavens present [10]
> Facets of Him who's veiled and immanent ;
>> Hence, O inquirer, learn what essence is,
>> What attribute, what cause, what consequent.]

Flash XXX

In some passages of the *Faṣūṣ* the Shaikh[11] (may God
show mercy upon him) seems to point to the view that the
existence of all contingent substances and of all perfections

---

[1] *Fiʻli* and *infiʻālī*, i.e. knowledge gained by inference and reasoning,
and that conveyed by immediate consciousness and sensation.

[2] *Wijdānī* and *dhauqī*.

[3] Here the last quatrain in Flash XXVIII is repeated.

[4] *Taqayyud*, limitation.

[5] The following passage in brackets is omitted in this manuscript.

[6] *Dhāt*.   [7] *Ṣifāt*.   [8] *Fiʻil* and *taʼthīr*.

[9] *Athār*.

[10] *Dunyā wa dīn*, earth and the celestial spheres, the " theatres " or
monstrances of the Divine perfections, rather than the world and the
Moslem Church (the ordinary meaning).

[11] See n. 4, p. 29.

dependent on that existence [¹ is to be ascribed to the
Majesty of the " Truth " most glorious and most exalted ;
whilst in other passages he seems to say that what is
ascribed to the Majesty of the " Truth " is merely an
emanation[2] of Being; and as regards the qualities
dependent on existence, they are effects produced by the
substances themselves. These two statements may be thus
reconciled : The Majesty of the " Truth " most glorious
is revealed in two manners—the first the inward, sub-
jective[3] revelation, which the Ṣūfīs name " Most Holy
Emanation ";[4] it consists in the self-manifestation of the
" Truth " to His own consciousness from all eternity under
the forms of substances,[5] their characteristics and capacities.
The second revelation is the outward, objective manifestation, which is called " Holy Emanation ";[6] it consists in
the manifestation of the " Truth ", with the impress of the
properties and marks of the same substances.[7] This second
revelation ranks after the first ; it is the theatre wherein
are manifested to sight the perfections which in the first
revelation were contained potentially in the characteristics
and capacities of the substances.

> One grace a host of suppliant forms designed,
> A second to each one his lot assigned ;
>> The first had no beginning—of the last,
> Which springs from it, no end can be divined.[8]

Wherefore, the ascription of existence and the
perfections dependent thereon] to the " Truth " most

---

¹ This passage in square brackets is found in one B.M. MS.   It
certainly makes the sense clearer.

² *Ifāzat*, production by emanation.   See De Sacy's article on "Jorjānī's
Definitions " (*Notices et Extraits des Manuscrits*, x, 66).

³ *'Ilmī*.

⁴ *Faiz i Aqdas* (see *Notices et Extraits*, x, 66), the first emanation, or
'aql i kull.

⁵ i.e. the " archetypal ideas " of the intelligible world, *'ālam i 'ilmī*.

⁶ *Faiz i Muqaddas*, the second emanation, or *nafs i kull* (*Anima mundi*).

⁷ i.e. *'ālam i 'ainī*, the sensible world, the copy of the intelligible world.

⁸ The sensible world issues from the intelligible world, and will
continue " as long as God wills "

glorious and most exalted has regard to the two
revelations taken together; and the ascription to the
"Truth" of existence alone, and of its dependents to the
substances, has reference to the second revelation; for
the only result of the second revelation is the emanation of Being into the substances, and so making visible
what had already been included in them by the first
revelation.

> Mark well this subtle point—each quality,
> Each action that in substances we see,
>   On one side is attributed to us,
> On one to "TRUTH", the sole Reality.

APPENDIX [1]

Whereas my aim and object in giving these explanations
and hints has been to call attention to the essential omnipresence of the Majesty of the "Truth" most glorious, and
to the immanence of His light in all the grades [of sensible
existence], to the end that the pilgrims and aspirants
endued with knowledge and reflection may not neglect the
contemplation of His Being while preoccupied with any
other being, and that they may not forget the consideration
of the perfection of His attributes while paying regard
solely to the qualities manifested [in the sensible universe],
and whereas what has been said above is sufficient for this
purpose, and satisfactorily accomplishes this end, I therefore conclude the book at this point, merely adding the
following quatrains:—

> Jāmī! leave polishing of phrases, cease
> Writing and chanting fables, hold thy peace;
>   Dream not that "Truth" can be revealed by words:
> From this fond dream, O dreamer, find release! [2]

[1] *Tadhyīl* in one manuscript; another has "Flash".
[2] The *Masnavī* finishes in the same strain. See the parable of the
Moslem who, by childlike faith, prevailed over his learned fellow-
travellers (p. 304).

Beggars in tattered clothes their rents should hide,
And lovers take discretion for their guide,

   And, since words do but veil the Loved One's face,
'Tis well for us in silence to abide.

How long wilt thou keep clanging like a bell ?
Be still, and learn this flood of words to quell ;

   Thou'lt never come to hold the pearl of " Truth "
Till thou art made all ear, as is the shell.[1]

Thou who for grief hast soiled thy weeds with dust,[2]
Soil not thy lips with speech (for soil it must);

   While thou canst commune silently with Him,
Rather than speak stop up thy mouth with dust !

   This treatise was completed by the help of God and the
favour of His grace.   May He bless Muhammad and his
family and his companions !

[1] i.e. the oyster-shell (see *Gulshan i Rāz*, l. 572).   Here in one manuscript there follow two quatrains which are mere variations of the
same theme.

[2] Read *Khākat ba kafan.*   v.l. *Chākat*, i.e. in token of mourning.

APPENDICES

APPENDIX I

GHAZĀLĪ ON THE UNITY AND ATTRIBUTES OF GOD[1]

PRAISE be to God, the Creator and Restorer of all things; who does whatsoever He pleases, who is Master of the glorious throne and mighty force, and directs His sincere servants into the right way and the straight path; who favoureth them who have once borne testimony to the Unity by preserving their confessions from the darkness of doubt and hesitation; who directs them to follow His chosen apostle, upon whom be the blessing and peace of God; and to go after his most honourable companions, to whom He hath vouchsafed His assistance and direction, which is revealed to them in His essence and operation by the excellencies of His attributes, to the knowledge whereof no man attains but he that hath been taught by hearing.[2] To these, as touching His essence, He maketh known that He is One, and hath no partner; singular, without anything like Him; uniform, having no contrary; separate, having no equal.[3] He is ancient, having no first; eternal, having no beginning; remaining for ever, having no end; continuing to eternity without any termination. He persists, never ceasing to be; remains without falling; and never did cease, nor ever shall cease, to be described by glorious attributes; nor is subject to any decree so as to be determined by any

[1] This passage is given in Pococke's *Specimen Historiæ Arabum* (Oxoniæ, 1650), p. 284, and this translation of it by Ockley is copied from Hughes's *Notes on Muḥammadanism*.

[2] "Faith cometh by hearing" (Rom. x, 17).

[3] This is directed against the Christian Trinity, which all Moslems suppose to be the equivalent of Tritheism.

precise limits or set times, but is the First and the Last, and is within and without.

What God is not.—He, glorified be His name, is not a body endued with form,[1] nor a substance circumscribed with limits or determined by measure ; neither does He resemble bodies, as they are capable of being measured and divided. Neither is He a substance, nor do substances exist in Him ; nor is He an accident, nor do accidents exist in Him. Neither is He like to anything that exists, nor is anything like to Him ; nor is He determinate in quantity, nor comprehended by bounds, nor circumscribed by differences of situation, nor contained in the heavens. He sits upon the throne, after that manner which He Himself hath described, and in that sense which He Himself means, which is a sitting far removed from any notion of contact, or resting upon, or local situation ; but both the throne itself, and whatsoever is upon it, are sustained by the goodness of His power, and are subject to the grasp of His hand.[2] But He is above the throne and above all things, even to the utmost ends of the earth ; but so above as at the same time not to be a whit nearer the throne and the heaven ; since He is exalted by (infinite) degrees above the throne, no less than He is exalted above the earth, and at the same time He is near to everything that hath being—nay, "nearer to men than their jugular veins, and is witness to everything"[3]— though His·nearness is not like the nearness of bodies, as neither is His essence like the essence of bodies. Neither doth He exist in anything,[4] neither doth anything exist in

[1] This is directed against the Anthropomorphists, the Kerāmians, and the Moshabbehites. See Sale, *Preliminary Discourse to Koran*, sect. viii.

[2] Just like Philo, Ghazālī struggles with the anthropomorphic language of the Koran in order to remove God from contact with matter, which his reading of Greek philosophy had taught him was evil.

[3] Surah 1, 15.

[4] Directed against those who held the doctrine of Incarnation, the Halūlians.

Him ; but He is too high to be contained in any place, and too holy to be determined by time; for He was before time and place were created, and is now after the same manner as He always was. He is also distinct from the creatures in His attributes, neither is there anything besides Himself in His essence, nor is His essence in any other besides Him. He is too holy to be subject to change or any local motion ; neither do any accidents dwell in Him, nor any contingencies before Him ; but He abides through all generations with His glorious attributes, free from all danger of dissolution. As to the attribute of perfection, he wants no addition. As to being, He is known to exist by the apprehension of the understanding ; and He is seen as He is by immediate intuition, which will be vouchsafed out of His mercy and grace to the holy in the eternal mansion, completing their joy by the vision of His glorious presence.[1]

His Power.— . . . His is the dominion and the excellency and the creation and the command.[2] . . . His excellency consists in His creating and producing, and His unity in communicating existence and the beginning of being.[3] . . .

His Knowledge.—He knows what is secret and conceals it, and views the conceptions of minds, and the motions of thoughts, and the inmost recesses of secrets by a knowledge ancient and eternal, that never ceased to be His attribute from eternal eternity, and not by any new knowledge superadded to His essence. . . .

His Will.—He doth will those things to be that are, and disposes of all accidents. Nothing passes in the empire or the kingdom, neither small nor great, nor good nor evil, nor profitable nor hurtful, nor faith nor infidelity,

---

[1] The beatific vision of Dante's Paradise. The idea came in the last resort from the Platonists, from whom Ghazālī also probably got it.

[2] Surah vii, 52, " Are not creation and command of Him ? "

[3] All created existence is one, and proceeds from the One.

nor knowledge nor ignorance, nor prosperity nor adversity, nor increase nor decrease, nor obedience nor rebellion, but by His determinate counsel and decree and His definite sentence and will. . . . He it is who gave all things their beginning; He is the Creator and Restorer, the sole Operator of what He pleases; there is no reversing His decree nor delaying what He hath determined; nor is there any refuge to man from his rebellion against Him but only His help and mercy; nor hath any man any power to perform any duty towards Him but through His love and will.[1]

His Word.—Furthermore, He doth command, forbid, promise, and threaten by an eternal ancient Word subsisting in His essence.[2]   Neither is it like to the word of the creatures, nor doth it consist in a voice arising from the commotion of the air or the collision of bodies, nor letters which are separated by the joining together of the lips or the motion of the tongue.   The Koran, the Law, the Gospel, and the Psalter are books sent down by Him to His apostles, and the Koran, indeed, is read with tongues, written in books, and kept in hearts; yet as subsisting in the essence of God it doth not become liable to separation and division when it is transferred to hearts and to papers.[3]   Thus, Moses also heard the word of God without voice or letter, even as the saints behold the essence of God without substance or accident. . . .

His Works.—He exists after such a manner that nothing besides Him hath any being but what is produced by His operation, and floweth from His justice after the best, most excellent, most perfect, and most just models. . . .[4]

[1] This language shows how easily the conception of Monotheism passed into Monism, i.e. the religious view into the philosophic.

[2] See Hirschfeld, *On the Qorān*, p. 14.   The *Logos*.

[3] This is the opinion that the Koran was uncreated, condemned by Al Mamūn in the second century A.H.   See Hirschfeld on the *I'jāz* (miracle) *of the Qorān*, p. 8.

[4] Here we have Plato's ideas or archetypes in the intelligible world, after the pattern of which sensible objects are formed.

All things were created by Him—genii, men, the devil, angels, heaven, earth, animals, plants, substance, accident, intelligible, sensible. He created them by His power out of mere privation, and brought them into light when as yet they were nothing at all,[1] but He Himself alone existed from all eternity, neither was there any other with Him. Now, He created all things in the beginning for the manifestation of His power and His will and the confirmation of His word, which was true from all eternity. Not that He stood in need of them, nor wanted them, but He manifestly declared His glory in creating and producing and commanding, without being under any obligation nor out of necessity. . . .

He rewards those that worship Him for their obedience on account of His promise and beneficence, not of their merit, nor of necessity, since there is nothing which He can be tied to perform ; nor can any injustice be supposed in Him ; nor can He be under any obligation to any person whatsoever. That His creatures, however, should be bound to serve Him ariseth from His having declared by the tongues of the prophets that it was due to Him from them. The worship of Him is not simply the dictate of the understanding, but He sent messengers to carry to men His commands and promises and threats, whose veracity He proved by manifest miracles,[2] whereby men are obliged to give credit to them in those things that they relate.[3]

[1] Privation, the Greek "not-being". Note also "substance" and "accident".

[2] Muḥammad's miracles were the *Āyāt*, signs (texts of the Koran). See Hirschfeld, *On the Qorān*, pp. 1, 8.

[3] Ghazālī speaks as an orthodox Moslem, but Greek influences are manifest in this passage, and his statements on the thorny subject of grace and works recall those of the great Christian Platonist Augustine.

APPENDIX II

PLOTINUS

FROM Anaxagoras down to the Stoics the main principle of Greek philosophy was Dualism, the opposition of the One and the many, of God and the universe of objects perceived by the senses.

Thus in an often quoted passage of the *Republic* Plato says " The ideal Good " (which in the *Timæus* he calls God) " is not existence (*ousia*), but is beyond existence ".

Next in the descending scale he placed the " Intelligible World " of Ideas or archetypes, conceived by intuitive reason (*Nous*). Then came the " Sensible World " of phenomena, which were only copies of the divine archetypes reproduced in matter.[1] This matter was of itself non-existent (*mē on*) ; in fact, a mere potentiality of taking the imprints of the archetypes.

With the Stoics monism made its appearance, and took the place of the previous dualism. For Plato's " Ideas " they substituted *Logoi*, thoughts, forms, or forces immanent in the universe. And these *Logoi* were often spoken of as all summed up in one *Logos*, or divine thought realized in the universe. Most Stoics, like Chrysippus, Cleanthes (quoted by St. Paul), and Marcus Aurelius, were theistic Monists, holding—*Jupiter est quodcunque vides, quocunque moveris.* Others were materialistic Monists, holding matter to be the one real substance, and the *Logoi* only functions of matter.

Philo, the Alexandrian Jew, who lived at the same time as St. Paul, managed to combine this *Logos* doctrine

[1] See *Masnavi*, p. 226.

with the Hebrew Scriptures.[1] By allegorical interpretation he identified the Stoic *Logoi* with the angels mentioned in the Scriptures, and at the same time he reduced the personal Yahveh of the Scriptures to the abstract Being of Greek philosophy. The Hebrew prophets had almost personified the " Word of the Lord " and " Wisdom "; and *Logos,* with its double meaning of thought and word (*ratio* and *oratio*), was easily identified with " Word " and " Wisdom ". As Dr. Hirschfeld has pointed out, *Amr* and *Kalima* underwent a similar process in the Koran.[2] The *Logos,* having been thus personified, plays a very important part in Philo's system. It becomes the Demiurge or Architect of the world. The metaphor of generation is employed to picture the mode of its operation. Sometimes it is figured as masculine, sometimes as a female agent (*epistēmē*), but in either case it is one of the parents of the world of phenomena.[3] On the whole it may be said that Philo's leading principles were, first, to remove the Deity far away from any contact with matter, and, secondly, to explain the existence of the world by the hypothesis of intermediate and subordinate agencies through whom the Deity worked, so as not to touch matter Himself.

Hence Philo's system was dualism. And this dualistic tendency was fostered by the growing influence of Manicheism. Manes, who formulated this old Persian dualism, did not live till the third century A.D., but many

[1] The Book of Wisdom, probably the work of a Hellenizing Jew, prepared the way for Philo, but the cautious writer speaks not of Greek "Logos", but of Hebrew "Wisdom", as the first effluent, the mirror and express image of the Deity (Wisd. vii, 26).

[2] *New Researches in the Qorān,* 1902, p. 15. Some Ṣūfī theologians identified Muhammad with " Universal Reason " or Logos. See Palmer's *Oriental Mysticism,* p. 43, and *Masnavī,* p. 179.

[3] Yonge's translation of Philo, i, 359, and ii, 205 (quoted in Appendix to *Masnavī*). Tholuck, when he encounters this idea in *Masnavī,* p. 77, and *Gulshan i Rāz,* l. 622, finds it shocking ; but few like to face the historical antecedents or parallels of cherished tenets.

of the Gnostic sects of the second century A.D. held what
were in fact Manichean opinions. And this led some,
like Basileides, to emphasize the separation of the Deity
from the evil material world. Basileides, for instance,
though he firmly believed in God, declared in hyperbolical
language that He was *ouk ōn*, " without existence," in the
sense of the phenomenal existence known to man.[1]
Others, like Valentinus, imagined a series of Æons or
intermediate Intelligences, so as to remove the transcendental God as far as possible from contact with
matter. These Æons were possibly the prototypes of the
Ṣūfī Ten Intelligences and of the Celestial Hierarchies of
Dïonysius, which supplied the frame of Dante's Paradise.

Plotinus, who lived in the third century A.D., was
a mystic who busied himself with philosophy only to seek
corroboration of his mystical beliefs. He started with the
conviction that the One was all in all, and that all
phenomena had no existence apart from it. He tried to
reach a conception of the transcendental One by abstracting
or stripping off all limitations and conditions incident to
phenomenal existence, and by assuming that the residuum
was the One. But as this residuum was void of all
positive contents, it could not be conceived by common
reason, and could be described only in negative terms,
as " Unconditional ", " Infinite ", " Incomprehensible "
(*immensus*), and the like. Reason could not say what it
was, but only what it was not. His position thus seems
to be precisely that of agnosticism, as expounded in
H. Spencer's *First Principles*. But here the resemblance
ceases. Plotinus held that the impotence of reason to
conceive the Absolute proved that ordinary reason must be
entirely discarded in these matters, so as to give free play
to the superior faculty of spiritual intuition or intuitive
reason (*Nous*), which alone is competent to deal with

---

[1] See Mansel's *Gnostic Heresies*, p. 147.

them.[1]   This faculty discerns the One to be no mere
negation, but a supreme energy of self-manifestation.[2]
Without any diminution or decrease of itself the One
ever pours forth or rays out effluences.   Hence arises an
image or reflection of the One in *Nous* or Reason, the First
Emanation, comprehending all being and all thought.
From this proceeded in like manner the Second
Emanation, called the " World-soul "[3] (*Psychē*), which
acted as the mediator between the supra-sensible and
the sensible worlds.   This, again, generated the particular
souls, human, animal, and vegetive, and, lastly, all inorganic
substances.   The substratum of all these manifestations
of the One in the sensible world was matter, which was
non-existent of itself (*mē on*) and yet the basis of each
sensible object (*bathos ekastou*),[4] in other words it was
a mere potentiality of receiving the imprint of the Divine
effluences.

The One, the Reason, and the World-soul constitute the
so-called Plotinian Trinity, which is one, not of equality
but of subordination.   Plotinus says Reason (*Nous*) is the
Logos of the One and Soul (*Psychē*) the *Logos* of the
Reason.[5]

So much for the theory.   As regards practice Plotinus
held that man's duty was to return to the One.[6]   The
motive for this return was the love of the divine spark in
his soul for its source, and its consequent craving to be

[1] Just so the Nominalists and their modern followers deny to reason
a voice, not only on questions of pure ontology, but on all points settled
by traditional dogma (Harnack, vi, 163) ; but thus to discard reason
altogether is to make every superstition impregnable.

[2] The scholastic term was "Actus purus", pure actuation or energizing.

[3] The later history of the " World-soul " is given in Renan's *Averroes*.
Dante censured it, and the Lateran Council of 1518 anathematized it.
Pope, following Spinoza, revived it.

[4] " Not-being " is an equivocal term—nothing in relation to God, but
a very pernicious something in relation to man.

[5] *Ennead*, v, 1, 6, quoted in Whittaker's *The Neoplatonists*, p. 37, n. 1.

[6] Plotinus followed Plato, who had said man's object should be to
attain likeness to God as far as possible (*Homoiōsis tō theō*).

reunited therewith. The One was itself unmoved, but attracted its effluents through being the object of their love and desire. The return was to be effected by retracing the downward course into the realm of matter. By what Dionysius later called the "negative way", the mystic aspirant must abstract and strip off all the material and sensuous accretions which had overlaid his real essence. This was to be effected,[1] first, by practising civic virtues, next the purifying virtues of asceticism and self-mortification, and finally the deifying virtue of contemplation.[2] At last he would transcend all the barriers separating him from the One, and would be absorbed and reunited with the One. Of this blessed state he could only hope to gain transient glimpses during life, but when the body perished he would abide for ever one with the One. Plotinus sums up by saying this is "the flight of the Alone to the Alone".

As Dr. Bigg points out, this mystical ascent of the soul is described by Augustine almost in the words of Plotinus :[3] "Thus as we talked and yearned after the eternal life, we touched it for an instant with the whole force of our hearts. We said, then, if the tumult of the flesh were hushed ; hushed ·these shadows of earth, sea, and sky ; hushed the heavens and the soul itself, so that it should pass beyond itself and not think of itself : if all dreams were hushed and all sensuous revelations, and every tongue and every symbol ; if all that comes and goes were hushed—they all proclaim to him that hath an ear : ' We

[1] This threefold division of the virtues agrees with the Ṣūfī division of the Law, the Path, and the Truth.

[2] Contemplation, *Theōria*, was *Theou orāsis*, the "beholding God", according to the Schoolmen's derivation of the word. Plotinus says the One is seen "in presence which is better than science" (*kata parousian epistēmēs kreittona*).

[3] See Bigg's *Confessions of St. Augustine*, p. 321 and note. All these Plotinian ideas were worked into Christian theology by Clement and Origen, himself a pupil of Ammonius Saccas, under whom Plotinus had studied. See Bigg's *Christian Platonists of Alexandria*.

made not ourselves ; He made us who abideth for ever.'—
But suppose that, having delivered their message, they
held their peace, turning their ear to Him who made
them, and that He alone spoke, not by them, but for
Himself, and that we heard His word, not by any fleshly
tongue, nor by an angel's voice, nor in the thunder, nor
in any similitude, but His voice, whom we love in these
His creatures—suppose we heard Him without any
intermediary at all—just now we reached out, and with
one flash of thought touched the Eternal Wisdom that
abides above all. Suppose this endured, and all other
inferior modes of vision were taken away, and this alone
were to ravish the beholder, and absorb him and plunge
him in mystic joy, might not eternal life be like this
moment of comprehension ? "

This is an admirable statement of the Plotinian "return"
to the One.[1] It also well illustrates the main characteristic of the system—viz., its ultimate dependence on
emotion rather than on intellect. Philosophy is only the
handmaid of theology, only used to support and justify
pre-existing beliefs. When his reason lands him in
contradictions, as it must do when it tries to transcend its
limits and outsoar the very atmosphere that bears it up,
Plotinus straightway falls back on feeling and the inner
light. Love and faith are a mighty spell, as Jalāl-ud-din
Rūmī says,[2] and with Plotinus love and faith are always at
hand to supplement the deficiencies of pure intellect.

The best accounts of Plotinus are those of Harnack in
his *History of Dogma*, English translation, i, 247 ; of Caird

---

[1] See Ghazālī's account in Appendix III. Also '*Hayy Ibn Yokdhan
or Philosophus autodidactus*, published by Pococke in 1671, and now
translated by Dr. Brönnle under the title *The Awakening of the Soul*
(Murray, 1905). See his Introduction, pp. 17–19. A passage of this is
quoted by the Quaker Barclay in his *Apology*, ed. of 1678, p. 126.
Plotinus's own account may be read in Thomas Taylor's translation
(Bell and Son's reprint, 1895, pp. 301–24).

[2] *Masnavi*, p. 262.

in his *Evolution of Theology in the Greek Philosophers*,
ii, 210 ; and of Whittaker in his *Neoplatonists*.   Opinions
differ as to whether he is to be classed as a Monist or as a
Dualist.   This would depend on whether his " not-being "
is to be regarded as nothing or as something.   Be this as
it may, no one can read his impassioned outpourings without seeing that his theological reasoned statements by no
means give the full measure of his beliefs.   What he did
believe in with a very passion of conviction was a Deity
endued in some sense with the principal attributes of
a personal God.

APPENDIX III

GHAZĀLĪ ON *FANĀ*, ANNIHILATION OF SELF OR ABSORPTION IN GOD[1]

" PRAYERS[2] have three veils, whereof the first is prayers uttered only by the tongue ; the second is when the mind, by hard endeavour and by firmest resolve, reaches a point at which, being untroubled by evil suggestions, it is able to concentrate itself on divine matters ; the third veil is when the mind can with difficulty be diverted from dwelling on divine matters. But the marrow of prayer is seen when He who is invoked by prayer takes possession of the mind of him who prays, and the mind of the latter is absorbed in God whom he addresses, his prayers ceasing and no self-consciousness abiding in him, even to this extent that a mere thought about his prayers appears to him a veil and a hindrance. This state is called "absorption" by the doctors of mystical lore, when a man is so utterly absorbed that he perceives nothing of his bodily members, nothing of what is passing without, nothing of what occurs to his mind—yea, when he is, as it were, absent from all these things whatsoever, journeying first *to* his Lord, then *in* his Lord. But if the thought occurs to him that he is totally absorbed, that is a blot ; for only that absorption is worthy of the name which is unconscious of absorption.

" I know these words of mine will be called an insipid discourse by narrow theologians, but they are by no means devoid of sense. Why ? The condition of which I speak is similar to the condition of the man who loves any other

---

[1] The Arabic text and a Latin translation of this passage are given by Tholuck in his *Sufismus*, pp. 3, 105.

[2] *Dhikr* is the term used to denote the orisons of the Dervishes.

things—e.g. wealth, honour, pleasures ; and, just as we see some engrossed by love, we see others overpowered by anger so that they do not hear one who speaks, or see one who passes, and are so absorbed by their overwhelming passion that they are not even conscious of being thus absorbed. For so far as you attend to the absorption of your mind, you must necessarily be diverted from Him who is the cause of your absorption. . . .

"And now, being well instructed as to the nature of 'absorption', and casting aside doubts, do not brand as false what you are unable to comprehend. God most high saith in the Koran : 'They brand as false what they do not comprehend.' The meaning of 'absorption' having been made clear, you must know that the beginning of the path is the journey *to* God and that the journey *in* God is its goal, for in this latter, absorption in God takes place. At the outset this glides by like a flash of light, barely striking the eye ; but thereafter, becoming habitual, it lifts the mind into a higher world, wherein the most pure essential Reality is manifested, and the human mind is imbued with the form of the spiritual world, whilst the majesty of the Deity evolves and discloses itself. Now, what first appears is the substance of angels, spirits, prophets, and saints, for a while under the veil of I know not what beautiful forms, wherefrom certain particular verities are disclosed ; but by degrees, as the way is opened out, the Divine Verity begins to uncover His face. Can anyone, I ask, who attains a glimpse of such visions, wherefrom he returns to the lower world disgusted with the vileness of all earthly things, fail to marvel at those who, resting content with the deceits of the world, never strive to ascend to sublimer heights ?"

A very similar doctrine is taught by the writer calling himself Dionysius the Areopagite, who has been recently identified with Stephen bar Sudaili, a Syrian monk.[1]

---

[1] Frotheringham, *Stephen bar Sudaili*, 1886.

He says the soul, following what he calls "the negative way" or method of abstraction, "after completing its ascent into that region of being which, from its very sublimity, is to the impotent human intellect a region of obscurity, becomes completely passive, the voice is stilled, and man becomes united with the Ineffable Being."[1] "Then is he delivered from all seeing and being seen, and passes into the truly mystical darkness of ignorance, where he excludes all intellectual apprehensions and abides in the utterly Impalpable and Invisible; being wholly His who is above all, with no other dependence, either on himself or any other; and is made one, as to his nobler part, with the utterly Unknown, by the cessation of all knowing; and at the same time, in that very knowing nothing, He knows what transcends the mind of man."[2] This is simply a restatement of the doctrine of Plotinus.[3]

[1] Ueberweg, *History of Philosophy*, Eng. trans., vol. i, p. 350.
[2] Vaughan, *Hours with the Mystics*, 2nd ed., vol. i, p. 287.
[3] Tholuck, *Blüthensammlung, Einleitung*, i, p. 6.

حامی تن زبان سخن طرازی جنید   اسنوا کری و فا ... نسازی جنبی

اظهار حقایق بسخن هیت خیال   ای سا ده ... ل ان خیال انی جنبی

درزنده و فقر عیب پوشی بهتر   درنکته عشق تیره هوشی بهتر

چون برخ مقصود نقاب بیفکن   از گفت و شنیده ما خموشی بهم

ما کی خود رای گردن افغان خوش   یکدم مشو از این هسر ورای خدا

گنجینه درهای حقایق نشوی   مادام که جو احد دف نکردی تمنی

ای گزنش انتاه و خاکت بین   آلوده مکن ضمیر پاکت بسخن

چون لال توان بود در و کریس   لب بکش بی نطق خاکت بین

تمت الرساله بعون الله
و حسن توفیقه و صلی الله
علی محمد و علی
آله و صحبه
اجمعین

نیست زیرا که مترتب نمیشود بر کلی یا فی الاضافه وجود در
اعیان و اظهار آنچه در اندراج یافته بود در ایشان مقتضی تجلی اول

بشنو سخنی مشکل و سری بعلتی	هر فعل و صفت که شد با عیانی حقی
از یک خبه آن جمله مضاف بما	اوز وجه دگر جمله مضاف بحقی

چون مقصود ازین عبارت و مطلوب ازین
اشارت ثبه بود و بر احاطهٔ ذات حق سبحانه و تعالی و بریز
نور او در جمیع مراتب وجود تا سالکان اکاه و طالبان حیا
اشباه بشهود هیچ ذات ازین مشاهد، جمال ذات غافل
نشوند و تظهر هیچ صفت از مطالعه کمالات صفات
غافل نگردند و الجه به کوشد در ادای این مقصود کا فی
بود و به پایان این مطلوب وافی لاجرم بدین قدر اقتضا
افتاد و بر این جذبه مبیت رباعی اختصار کرد و شد

ودرضمن فعلی وانفعالی عینی و انفعالی و درضمن علم ذوقی و وجدانی عین علم ذوقی و وجدانی تا غایتی که درضمن علم موجو د اتی که بحسب عینہ ایشانرا عالم مینامند عین علمیت که لاینحال البتہ وعلی هذا لبیا پس سایرالصفات والکمالات

وار و پسران دربهمہ عین اعیان	هستی بصفا پیتے که در وبو ونهان
بہ قدقبول عین کشتست عیان	مروصف زریغی بود قابل آن
او صاف تو درصفاتشان متواری	ای ذات تو درذوات اعیان
ورضمن مظاہراز نیدیعساری	وصفہ تو وجو ذات مطلق آنست

کلام شیخ رضی الله عنہ دربعضی مواضع فصوص مشعر آنست که وجو د اعیان ممکنات وکمالات البہ مو جو د را بحق سبحانه و تعالی باعتبار مجموع تجلیاپ ست واضافہ وجو د بحق واضافہ توابع آن بایسان باعتبار کلی

اِنَّا بَعَثْنَا لِلْوُجُودِ فِی الْمَوْجُودَاتِ بَاسِرُها

هستئ بصفاتی که در و بود نهان	دار دِ سپرﯾان دِهِمَا عیانِ جهان
سر وصف زِ عینی که بود قابل آن	برقد رقبول عین گشتست عیان ۷

همچنانکه حقیقت هستی از جهت صرافت اطلاق
خودش مباشر یت در ذوات جمع موجودات بخشی که در آن
ذوات عین آن ذواتست چنانکه آن ذوات در وی
عین بود و همچنین صفات کامله او وکلیاتها و اطلاق ها
در جمیع صفات موجودات ساری اند بنابه که در ضمن
صفات ایشان عین صفات ایشا ندچنانکه صفات
ایشان و عین آن صفات کامله عین آن صفات کامله
بود و ند مثلا صفت علم در ضمن علم عالم بجزو یات عین
علم بجزو یاتست و در ضمن علم عالم بکلیات عین علم بکلیات

اما علم بر دو وجهت یکی آنکه بحسب عرف ازآن علم میکویند و دیگر
آنک بحسب عرف ازآن علم نمیکویند و هر دو قسم مشارالیه
حقیقت از مقوله علم است زیرا که ایشان شاهد می کنند
سرایت علم ذاتی حق را سبحانه در جمیع موجودات و آنز
قبیل قسم ثانی آنست مثلاک بحسب عرف اورا عالم نمی آند
اما می بینم اورا که تمیز میکند میان بلندی و پستی از بلندی عدول
میکند و بجانب پستی جاری میکند و و سخن و و دراخل می نخیل
نفوذ میکند و ظاهر جسم مکاثف را تر طیب میکند و میکند
آی عزیز ذلک پس از خاصیت علم است جریان می بر
مقتضای قابلیت قابل و عدم مخالفت با آن اما در این
مرتبه علم در صورت طبعت ظاهر شده است و علی هذا القیاس
سرایه العلم فی سایر المو جودات بل سرایه جمیع الکمالات

وتفاوت علم بحسب تفاوت حقایقت درقبول نه
وجود کمال ا و نقصان پس آنکه قابلست مرهجو درا علی الوجه
الاتم لاکمل قابلست مرعلم را علی هذا الوجه وآنکه قابلست
مرهجو درا علی الوجه الانقص تصفت علی هذا الوجه ومنشا
این تفاوت غالبیت ومغلوبیت احکام وجوب
وامکانست دربه حقیقت که احکام وجوب غالبتر انجاوجه
علم کاملتر و دربه حقیقت که احکام امکان غالبتر وجود و
علم ناقص تر وغالبا که خصوصیت حکم تابعیت علم مرهجو را
که درکلام شیخ واقعست برسبیل تمثیل است والاجمیع
کمالات تابه مرهجو در این حین و قدرت و ارادت
وغیرها همین است وقال بعضهم قدس سر الله تعالی
اسرارهم سبب درهر موجودات از صفت علم عاری

از بین جهت است که کیفیت است از کیفیات زیرا که او از بین
جهت کمالی است از کمالات بلکه از آن جهت که سبب
شده است مر عدم وصول ثمار را بکمالات لایعدو خود
و همچنین قیل مثلا که شربت شربیت او نه از جهت قدرت
قابلیت بر قتل او قاطعیت آلت یا قابلیت عضو مقتول
مقطع را بلکه از جهت زوال حیات است و آن امر نسبت
عدمی سیأتی غیر ذلک من الامثله

هر جا که وجود کرده سیرت ای دل	میدان تعین که محض حیرت ای دل
هر شر ز عدم بود عدم غیر وجود	پس شر همه مقتضای غیرت ای دل

شیخ صدرالدین قونوی قدس الله تعالی سره
در کتاب نصوص می‌فرماید که علم تابع است مروه و را
آن معنی که هر حقیقت از حقایق را که وجود هست علم هست

چون صفات و احوال و افعال که درمظان حاضر

فی الحقیقة مضاف بحق طاهر دران مظاهر ست پس اگر احیانا

دربعضی ازانها شری و نقصانی واقع باشد ازجهة عدمیت

امری دیگر توانند بود زیراک وجود من حیث هو وجود خیر

محض ست و از سرا امری وجودی که شری متوهم میشود

بواسطة عدمیت امر وجودی دیگر ست نه بواسطة آن

امر وجودی من حیث هو امر وجودی

باشد زعنوت ذات پاک بینا	بشد زعنوت ذات پاک بینا	سرنگ ازقبل خیر ست کمال
دار دقصور قابلیات مآل	درحبا به شرست دو بال	هر حبہ کہ درحبا به شرست دو بال

حکما دراینک آن وجه خیر محض ست دعوی ضرورت

کرده اند و ازبرای توضیح مثالی چند آورده اند وگفتہ کہ

بجز مثلا متلف شمائیت و شرست نسبت باثمار اوند

فی الحقیقة از حق ظاهر در آن مظاهر ظاهر است به رسبت نه از مظاهر

شیخ رضی الله عنه در حکمت علیه میفرماید لا فعل للعبد بل الفعل لربها فیها فاطانت الیین ان یضاف الیها

پس نسبت فعل بنده از رتبه ظهور حقیقت بصورت او نه نه از جهت نفس او

مینوان وجود

و قدرت و فعل خود را از حضرت بچون میدان

از مامه عجز و بستی مطلوبست	هستی و توان عیش زها بسته
این اویت بدید آمد در صورت تعلق	این قدرت و فعل از آن به مشتق
چون ذات تو منفی بود واهی کبیش	از نسبت افعال نجو بازکش
شیرست کشی شنو کمن وی بیش	ثبت للعبد اولایثم آن فش
وصافی خود بر عم حاتمکی	ترویج چنین متاع کامدکی
تو سعد و می خیال هستی از تو	فاسد باشد خیال فاسدکی

آنچه موجود و مشهود پست حقیقت وجود پست اما باعتبار
تلبس باحکام و آثار اعیان نه از حیثیت تجرد از آنها زیرا کاران
حیثیت بطون و خفا از لوازم او پس فی الحقیقت
وجود همچنان بر حقیقت خود پست بر وحدت حقیقی خود
که از آن لا بود و ما دا خواهد بود اما بنظر اغیار بسبب احتجاب
بصورت کثرت احکام و آثار متقید و متعین
در می آید و متعدد و متکثر می نماید

زان بحر پدیده غیر موج ایمن جهان	بحریت وجود جاودانست زمان
بر ظاهر بحر حبس نحو در موج نهان	از باطن بحر موج بین کشف عیان
درین عمر	متکی بو ذات خداوندگر
با شد همه چیز مندرج در حمه	اثنیت بمان از این عارف گوید

در قدرت و فعل کز ظاهر ازمظاهر صادر می نماید

تخمین مسافتی از عبارات محبی   بی رفع قیود و اعتبارات محبی

خواهی بیای زعلت جبل ثقیل   تا نون نخابت از اشارات محبی

کشتی بتوقف بر موافق قانع   شد قصد مقاصدت بمعقده طالع

هرگز نشود تا کنی رفع حجب   انوار خفیت از مطالع طالع

در رفع حجب گوش ده در رجع کتب   که جمع کتب نمیشود رفع حجب

در طی کتب کجا بود شاهد حب   طی کن همه را و خدا الی القه بطلب

عظیم ترین حجابی و کثیف ترین نقابی جهل و حدت حیثیتی رائید

و تعقد داشتست که در ظاهر وجود واقع شد و است بواسطه

نبس آن باحکام و آثار و اعیان ثابته در حضرت علم که باطن

وجود پست و مجرد با نواحیان می نماید که اعیان موجود شد

در خارج و حال آنکه بویی از وجود خارجی نشام ایشان

نرسیده است و همیشه در عدمیت خود بوده اند و خواهند بود

مراین اعراض را واگذار یا رب نظر میکنید که امثال

این منهومات فصول نبیشد بلکه لوازم فصولند که بان از

فصول تعبیر میکنند بواسطه عدم قدرت بر فضول تقسیم

از حقایق فصول بر وجهی که ممتاز شود نمار از ماعدای خود بنبر این

لوازم با لوازم چه که از بنها اخفی باشد مقدمه ایست ممنوع

کلام است نا مسموع و بر تقدیر تسلیم هر چه نظر با جوهر ذاتی

باشد قیاس آن بعین واحد عرضی خواهد بود زیرا که هر چه داشت

در حقیقت خارجت از ان عین واحد و قائم است با وجود عوی

اینک آنجا امری هست جوهری و رای عین واحد در غایت

پستوطیت بتخصیص وقتی که کشف ارباب حقیقت که منتقل

از مشکن نبوت بخلاف آن که اسی و عده و مخالف

حاجز با شد از آن از اقامت دلیل

یل بر ابکه مجموع اعراض مجتمعه است در عین واحد که حقیقت

وحود است آنکه هر چند حقایق موجود ذات ممکن را تجدد میکنند

در حد و ذات ایشان غیر از اعراض حسیّه ی ظاهر نمیشود مثلا وقتیکه

که بیند انسان حیوان ناطقیت وحیوان جسم نامی حساس

متحرک بالاراده وجسم جوهر قابل ابعاد ثلثه وجوهریت

لانی موضوع وموجود ذاتیّت که مرا و راتحقق وحصول

باشد در این حد و در چه مذکور میشود از قبیل اعراضیت

الا آن ذات بسبب که در این مفهومات ملحوظیت زیراکه

معنای طق ذات لا النطق است ومعنای ذات

لا النمو وهکذا لا ابواقی واین ذات مبهم عن وجود

حقیقتی حتمی است که قایمت بذات خود و متقومت

مقتضی اصمحلال تعینات و آثار کثرت صوری است
از ان تعین منسلخ گردد و در همان آن انسلاخ بر تمقضای
رحمت رحمانیه تعینی دیگر خاص که مماثل تعین سابق باشد
متعین گردد ، و در آن ثانی بتقدیر احدیت مضمحل گردد و تعیّنی
دیگر بر رحمت رحمانیه حاصل و هکذا الی ما شاء الله، پس
در هیچ دو آن یک سبک تجلی واقع نشود و در سرای غیر املی
بعدم رود و دیگری مثل آن بوجود آید اما موجب عجب
تعاقب امثال و تناسب احوال می پندارد که وجود عالم
بر یک حالت است و در ازمنه متوالیه بر یک منوال

در سر نفسی متجلیست بتجلی دیگر و در تجلی او اصلا مگر او نیست یعنی

ور در آن یک تعین و یک شان متجلی نمیگردد بلکه در هر نفسی

بتعین دیگر ظاهر میشود و در سر آنی شانی و یکی بتجلی میگیرد د

درشان درک جلوه کبت آن الهی	مستی عیان هست در آن درشانی
گر بایدت از کلام حق بانی	این نکته بجز کل بوم نشانی

وسه در این آنست که حضرت حق را اسماست متقابله

بعضی لطیفه و بعضی قهریه و همه دایما بر کار زند و تعطیل رنج

یک جا نیز پس هر چه هستی از حقایق امکانیه بواسطه حصول

شرایط و ارتفاع موانع مستبعد وجود کرد در حت رحمانیه

اورا در یابد و بر وی افاضه وجود کند و ظاهر وجود بواسط

لبس آثار و احکام آن حقیقت متعین کرد و بتعینی خاص

متجلی شو و بحسب آن تعین بعد از آن بسبب قهر احدیت حقیقی

بحریست نه کاهنده نه افزا | امواج پرورنده و آبنده

عالم جوعبارت از همین امواج | نبود و دو زمان لَیک دوان

عالم بود ارنه زعبرت عاری | جهری جاری بطورها ساری طاری

و ندر همه طورهای جمع جاری | سِرِّیست حقیقة الحقائق ساری

و اما خطاء سوفطائیه آنست که مع قولهم بالتبدل الیی فی العالم باسره متنبه نشده اند بانک یک حقیقت که متلبس میشود بصور و اعراض عالم وموجودات متعیّنه متعدّده می نماید وظهور فت او را در مراتب کونی جمیزِ این صور و اعراض خیالک وجود نیت در خارج بدون او

سوفطائی که ازخرد پنجر پت | گوید عالم جز لا الی اند رکهت

آری عالم همه خیال است ولی | پیوسته در و حقیقتی جلوه گر پت

و اما ارباب کشف و شهود می بینند که حضرت حق سبحانه و

لا يبقى زمانين و مكرّ چپ با یہ که معروفند بسوفطا ئیہ درجملہ احزاى

عالم جہ جواہرو چہ اعـراض و ہریک از فرزقین من وجہی

خطا کرده اند اما اشاعرہ سبب آنکہ اثبات جواہر متعدّد

کرده اند ورای حقیقت وجود و اعراض متبدلہ متّحدہ

را بآنها قائم داشتہ و ندانستہ اند کہ عالم مجموع اجزاء

بیست کہ اعراض متّجدّدہ متبدّل مع الانفاس کرد

درعین واحد جمع شدہ اند و درہرآنی از ین عین زایل

پیشوند و امثال انها بوی ملتبس بس مکرر و ندیدہ ناظر باطل

تعاقب امثال درغلط می افتد و می پندارہ دان ست آنکہ

واحد مستمر کما یقول الاشـاعـرۃ فی تعاقب الامثال علی

محل الغرض من عنہ خلوان من شخص من العـ ہ ضہ ماثل

لشخص الاول نظیر الناظـر انها امر واحد مستمر

واحدیت از انب واعتبارات اسماء هوالاول والاخر والظاهر والباطن

لا بلکه عین است همه آفاق	برشکل تابان روز غیبی است
والله که همان زر روی طلاق	چیزی که بود زر روی تقید جهان
مشهود مشاهدان عالم مریو دوریا	چون حق تعالی شیود کشف عیان
با رتبه اجمال حق آید بیان	کرا ز رو عین عالم و عالیان

شیخ رضی الله عنه در فص شیبی میفرماید که عالم

عبارتست از اعراض مجتمعه در عین واحد که حقیقت هستی

وان متبدل و متجدد می کرد د مع الانفاس عین الانات

در ثانی عالم بعدم میرود و مثل آن بوجود می آید واکثر

اهل عالم از این معنی غافلند کما قال سبحانه

وازا رباب نظر کسی بر این مطلع نشست

مگر اشلمه و راجزای عالم که اعراض است حیث قالوا الاعا

همهٔ اشیاست واو نی جهت ذات و احدیت که عدد را بار واه
نیست اما باعتبار تجلیات تکثر و تعینات متعدده در
مراتب تأثر حقایق جوهریه متنوعه است و بنابراین حقایق
عرضیه تا بعد پس ذات واحد بواسطه متعدد جواهر واعراض
تکثر می نماید و من حیث الحقیقت که اصلاً متعدد و مکثر نیست

پندارد و یی دلیل پیش اینست غلط	ای بر سر حرف این و آن ازدخط
یک عین و جب دار یک دانه فقط	در جمله کائنات بی سهو و غلط

این عین واحد از حیثیت تجرد و اطلاق از تعینات و تقیدات
مذکوره حیثیت و از حیثیت تعدد و تکثری که بواسطهٔ تلبس
او تعینات می نماید خلق و عالم پس عالم ظاهر حیثیت و حق
باطن عالم من از ظهور عین حق بود و حق غیب از ظهور
عین عالم لکن فی الحقیقه یک حقیقت و ظهور و بطون اولیت

تجلی اوست بر خود و صور حقایق و اعیان ممکنات پس فی الحقیقة وجود یکی ثر نیست که در جمیع این مراتب و حقایق متفرته در آن ساری است و وی در این مراتب و حقایق عین این مراتب و حقایق است چنانکه این مراتب و حقایق در وی عین وی بود و از این حیث

	هستی که ظهور میکند در جمیع اشیا	خواهی که بری حجال بی ها پرده پس
روی سمای حجاب را گشا پنا	می می بود و اندر روی روی می می
بر لوح عدم لوایح قدم	لایح گردید و کس از من پنهم محرم

| چون آدم است |
| حق را مشمر جدا از عالم زیرک | عالم در حق حق است و حق در عالم |
| جزء عالم است |

حقیقة الحقایق که ذات الهی است تعالی شانه ثابت است

مرتبهٔ ثانیه تعین اوست و تعین بتعین تابع مرجع تعینات فعلیه وجوبیه

آنیه را و جمیع تعینات انفعالیه امکانیه که نیه را و این مرتبه سمّا

تعین اول زیرا که اول تعینات حقیقت وجود اوست و فوق

او مرتبهٔ لاتعیت لا مرتبهٔ غیر ثابتهٔ احدیت جمع جمیع تعینات

فعلیه مؤثره است و این مرتبهٔ الوهیت است مرتبه را بتفضیل

مرتبهٔ الوهیت و مرتبهٔ اسما و حضرت ایشان است و اعتبار

این دو مرتبه از حیثیت ظاهر و وجود است که و جرب و صف و

خاص اوست مرتبهٔ خامسه احدیت جمع جمیع تعینات

انفعالیه است که از شان اثبات اثاره و انفعال لان

مرتبه که نیه امکانیه است مرتبه با و بتفضیل مرتبه که نیه

امکانیه است که مرتبه عالم است و عوض این دو مرتبه

باعتبار طاهره علمت که امکان ازلو ازم اوست و آن

وصفات و مقدس است از دلالت الفاظ و لغه و نقل را درنعت جلال او و زبان عبارتست و عقل البکه کمال و مکان اشارت هم ارباب کشف از ادراک حقیقتش درحجاب و نیم اصحاب علم از ابداع نقش و اضطراب غایت نشان از و بی نشان مبهت و نهایت عرفان وی حیرانی

ای و توعیا نها و نها نها مه سج	پندار تیها و کانها مه سج
بر ذات تو مطلقا نشان ژوان وار	کانجا که توی مو دنش نها مه سج
مه چند که جان عارف آگاه بود	کی در حرم قدست واش را بود
دست بیه اهل کشف ار بابه بود	از دامن ادراک تو کوتاه بود
این عشق هست خزو لا نیک	جانثا که شو و عقل ما مدرک
خوش اکه زنو راود مه صبح نقین	ما را برما نذار ظلام شک

ونسبت و اعتبارات مخصوصه است که درسایر مراتب
نیست چون مرتبه الوهیت و ربوبیت و مرتبه بعودیت
وخلقیت پس اطلاق اسامی مرتبه آلهیت مثلا چون الله
و رحمن و غیر هما بر مراتب که نیه عین کفر و محض زندقه باشد
وهمچنین اطلاق اسامی مخصوصه بمراتب که نیه بر مرتبه
آلهیت غایت ضلال و نهایت خذلان باشد ٠

وندرصنعت صدق وصفینی	ای برده کاک صاحب تحتی
کر حفظ مراتب نکنی لیق	هرمرتبه از وجو دبسکمی دارد

موجو د جیتی کی شن نیست و آن عین وجود حقا
ومتی مطلق است اما او را مراتب بسیار است اول
مرتبه لا تعین و عدم انخصار است و اطلاق از سر قیبه
واعتبار از این حیثیت منزه است از اضافت نعوت

تعیّن بهان شان در مان حضرت، واثیاء موجوده

عبارت اذا از تعیّنات وجود با عتبار انصلاخ ظاهر

وجود با آثار واحکام حقایق اشان یا خود وجود متعیّن

بهین اعتبارات بروجهی که حقایق منثه در باطن وجود

پنهان بابشند واحکام وآ ثار ایشان وظاهر بروجود پدید

زیرا که زوال صور علمیه از باطن وجود مجالست والا

جهل بازم آید

در خارج و ، علم عارض ذات وجود	یا بهر وجهه واعتبارات وجود
طاهر شده بعکس زمرات وجود	ورپراز ظلمت علم مستویم

حقیقت وجود اگر برجمیع موجودات ذهنی

وخارجی مشتمل ومتحول میشو دامااورا مراتب متفاوتست

و در هرمرتبه اورا اسامی وصفات

هر کس که نباشد تو عوض باشدِ او را | و آن را که نباشی تو کسی نیست عوض

استغنای مطلق از مقید باعتبار ذاتست و الاظهور اسماء الوبت
و تحقق نسب ربوبت بی مقید از محالاتست

ای باعث شوق و طلبم خوبئ تو | فرع طلب منست مطلوبئ تو
گر آینه محبئ من نمود | ظاهر نشو جمال محبوبئ تو

لا بلکه هم محب حقتست و هم محبوب او و هم طالب حقتست
و هم مطلوب او مطلوب و محبوبت در مقام جمع احدیت
و طالب و محبت در مرتبه تفصیل و کثرت

ای غیر ترا بسوی تو تپریئ | حائی ز تو سجده هئ می آرائی
دیدم همه طالبان تو یسی و در میان عین تئی | آن جمله طالبان و مطلبارا

حقتست سرمئی یقین و جود ست در حضرت
علم باعتبار شانی که آن سینئ منظهر او ست یا ز و وجود

مطلق سے مقید نباشد و مقید بی مطلق

صورت نہ بندد اما مقید محتاج ست بمطلق و مطلق

مستغنی از مقید پس استلزام از ظرفیت و احتیاج از

یک طرف خبا کہ میان حرکت ید و حرکت مقماح کہ دید

ای درحرم قدس کوتر راجانی	عالم تو پیدا و تو خود پیدائی
و تو نیم جدائیم آست پ	مارا تو حاجت فذرا اہانی

و ایضاً مطلق مستلزم مقید ست و مقید ست از مقیدات علی سبیل

البدلیہ نہ مستلزم مقید مخصوص و چون مطلق ابدی ست

فلذا احتیاج ہمہ مقیدات اوست لاغیر

قرب تو با سباب و علت شوان ست	ای سابقہ فضل ازل شوان ست
مہر کہ بود و توان کردن بہ	نوی مدی ترا بدل شوان ست
ای ذات رفیع تو نہ جوہر عرض	فضل کرمت نیست معلل غرض

ظهور و خفای شئون و اعتبارات بسبب تلبس

بظاهر وجود و عدم آن موجب تغیّر حقیقت وجود و صفات

حقیقیهٔ او نیست بلکه مبنی بر تبدّل نسب و اضافاتست و آن

مقتضی تغیّر در ذات نی آنکه عمرو از یمین زید برخیزد و بر

یسار ش نشیند نسبت زید با او مختلف شود و ذاتش با

صفات حقیقیهٔ خود بهمان برقرار و همچنین حقیقت وجود

بواسطهٔ تلبس بامور شریفه به زیادتی کمال کبریا و حیثیت

ظهور مظاهر خسیسه به نقصان نپذیرد و نور آفتاب به چند

بر پاک و پلید با بی هیچ تغیّر میاباطت نورت او را نیاید

نه از مشک بوی گیرد و نه از گل زنگ نه به خار عار و نه از جار اننگ

جون خور فروغ ونغ خود جهانید   بر پاک و پلید اگر تابد شاید

نی نور وی از هیچ پلیدآلاید   نی پاکی از آن هیچ پاک افزاید

مراد باندراج کثرت یشون در وحدت

ذات نه اندراج جزو پست در کل یا اندراج مظروف

در ظرف بلکه مراد اندراج اوصاف و لوازمست بوجو

و ملزوم عین اندراج نصفیت و ثلثیت و ربعیت حیثیت

آلی ما لانهایة له در ذات واحد عددی زیرا که این سب

در روی مندرجند و اصلا لاظهور ندارند ما دام که تکرار

طور در مراتب جزو و اثنین و ثلثه و اربعه و خمسه واقع نشود

و از اینجا معلوم میشود که احاطه حق سبحانه و تعالی جمیع

موجو دراتست مجو احاطه ملزو مست بلوازم نه بچون احاطه کل کرو

بالعرف بهظروف تعالی الله لایلیق بجناب قدسه

در ذات حق اندراج شان سروو	شاهد حسن صفتت ذوات حسنوو
این قاعده یاد دار کانجا که خدا	نه جزو و کل نه ظرف نه مظروفت

وخواه تعینات و تشخصات همه شئون الهی اند که مندرج

و مندمج بوذند در وحدت ذات اولا در مرتبه علم بصورت

اعیان ثابته برآمدند و ثانیا در مرتبه عین بواسط تلبس

احکام و آثار ایشان نظا مروجو د که مجلی آئینه است

مر باطن وجو در اصورت اعیان خارجیه کر فشد پس نیست

در خارج الاحقیقی واحد که بواسط تلبس پشئون و صفات

متبکثره و متعدد می نما ید نسبت بآنان که درحین مراتب

مجبوس اند و باحکام و آثار آن مقید

مجموعه کون را تاکنون نسق حقا که ندیدیم و نخواندیم درو	کردیم تصفح ورقابعد ورق جزذات حق و شئون ذاتیه حق
ناچند حدیث جسم وابعاد و جها یک ذات فقط بود و منی شئونست و صفا	ناکی سخن معدن و حیوان و نبا این کثرت و منی شئونست وصفا

و آنچه با او در تحت جسم نامی مندرجست رفع کنی همه در جسم

نامی جمع شوند و چون ممیزات جسم نامی را و آنچه را او مندرج

تحت الجسم رفع کنی همه در حقیقت جسم جمع شوند و چون

ممیزات جسم را و آنچه با او مندرجست تحت الجویه یعنی

العقول و النفوس رفع کنی همه در حقیقت جو مر جمع شوند و چون

با به الامتیاز ممکن بُوَد واجبَ را جوهر و عرض را رفع کنی

همه در تحت ممکن جمع شوند و چون، به الامتیاز ممکن قوّا

را رفع کنی مر وجود در موجود مطلق جمع شوند که عین حقیقت

وجود است و بذات خود موجود است نه بوجود زاید

بر ذات خود و وجوب صفت ظاهر اوست و امکان

صفت باطن او اعنی الاعیان الثابته الحاصله بتجلیه علی

نفسه مبدأ بشوند و این ممیزات خواه فصول و خواص

وتشابه فى المراتب و ازين حيثيت از وجود جمع

موجودات مستغنيت كما قال سبحانه ان الله لغنى عن العالمين

وامان غناى عشق پاك امدك	زآلودكى نياز ايشنى خاك
چون جلوه كر و نظار كى جمله خود	كرما و تو درميان نباشيم خبر
هرشان و صفت كه مستى حق دارد	درخود همه معلوم مخفى دارد
درضمن مقيدات محتاج بخود	از ديدن آن غناى مطلق وارد
واجب ز وجود نيك و بد مستغنيت	در خود همه را جاودان مند
واحد ز مراتب عدد مستغنيت	از ديدنشان بربون زخود مستغنيت

چون تشخصات و تعينات افراد و انواع

مند ر جذتخت الكحو انرا رفع كنى افرا دهـر نوعى در دى

جمع شوند و چومميزات آن انواع را كه فصول و خواص

رفع كنى همه در حقيقت حيوان جمع شوند و چون مميزات حيوان

وشهادت چه در دینی و چه در آخرت و مقصد ما اینها

تحقیق ظهور کمال اسمائیست که کمال جلا واستجلاست کمال

جلا یعنی ظهور را و بحسب این اعتبارات و کمال یعنی استجلا

شود و او هم بحسب همین اعتبارات و این ظهور و شهود

عیانی یعنی جون ظهور و شهود بجمله مفصل بخلاف کمالی که این ظهور

ذاتیست منفس خود را از برای نفس خودبی اعتبار غیریه

و غیریت و این ظهور ست علمی جون ظهور مفصل مجمل

و غنای مطلق لازم کمال ذاتیست و معنی غنای مطلق ست که

شیون واحوال واعتبارات ذات با حکمها و لوازمها

علی وجه کلی بجمله که در جمله مراتب حقایق آلهی و کونیه

می نماید مرذات را زمطرنها و اندراج الکل فی وحدتها

مشاهده و ثابت باشند بجمیع صورها واحکامها کاظهر ثست

ازینکه کثر وصور معلومیت ذات متلبسة بهند والاعتبار

حقائق کونیة است و تلبس ظاهر وجود با حکام و آثار اینها

موجب تعدد وجود است و بعضی از ان حقائق که اینها

عند سریان الوجود فیها ، با حدیتیه جمع شؤنه و ظهور آثارها

و احکامها به استعدا د ظهور جمع اسماء آیست سوی

او بر حسب الذاتی علی اختلاف المراتب الظهور شدةً

و ضعفا و غالبیته و مغلوبیته چون کل افراد انسانی از اینها

و اولیا و بعضی را استعدا د ظهور بعضیت دون بعضی

علیٰ اختلاف المذکور چون سایر موجودات حضرت

ذات با حدیتیه جمع شؤنها الٰهیه و الکونیه ازلاً و ایداً جمع

این حقایق که تفاصیل مرتبه واحدیة اند سارست و متجلی

چه در عالم ارواح وچه در عالم مثال وچه در عالم حس پس

بطون واولیت و ازلیت و باعتبار اتصاف الوالحج
صفات و اعتبارات مرتبهٔ واحدیت و ماوراء است
ظهور و آخریت و ابدیت و اعتبارات مرتبهٔ واحدیت
بعضی از ان قبلند که اتصاف ذات بانها باعتبار مرتبه
جمعیت خواه مشروط باشند تحقق وجوه و بعض حقایق
کونیه چون خالقیت و رازقیت و غیرهما و خواه نباشند
چون حیایت و علم و اراده و غیرها و اینها اسما و صفات الهیت
و بر وبهن اند و صورت معلومیت ذات متلبسه
بهذه الاسماء و الصفات حقایق آلهیه است و لمتبر ظاهر
وجود بانها موجب تعدد وجودی نیست و بعضی از ان قبلند
که اتصاف ذات بانها باعتبار مراتب کونیه است
چون فصول و خواص و تعینات که ممیزات اعیان خارجیه اند

ظاهر نور ، و ظهور باسپسال ستور و خفای او با عتبار صرافت

و اطلاق ذاتیت و ظهور باعتبار مظاهر و تعینات

بکلخ خویش کنم ای غنچه دنیا	هر لحظه بپوشم جه حسن تو نهان
زو خنده که منی بعکس خوبان جهان	در پرده عیان باشم و بینی پرده
رخسار تو بی نقاب دیدن نتوان	دیدار تو بی حجاب دیدن نتوان
ماد ام که در کمال اشراق نور د	سرچشمه آفتاب دیدن نتوان
خورشید چو بر فلک زدد رایت نور	در پرتو او خیره شود دیده
و اندم که کنی زبیرده انظر صور	فالناظر بجلیه من غیر قصور

یقین اول و حدتیت صرف و قابلیتیت

محض مشتمل بر جمیع قابلیات چه قابلیت تجرد و از جمع اعتبارات

و صفات و چه اتصاف همه و باعتبار تجرد و از جمع اعتبارات

باغایتی که از قابلیت این تجرد نیز مرتبه احدیت و او است

ذات من حیث هی از همه اسماء و صفات معرّاست

و از جمیع نسب و اضافات مبرّا انقیاف او باین امور

باعتبار توجّه اوست بعالم ظهور در تجلّی اوّل که خود کو برخ

نمود و نسبت علم و لوازم وجود و شهود و متحقق کشت و نسبت علم

و نسبت علم مقتضی عالمیّت و معلومیّت شد و در مستلزم ظهور

و ظاهریّت و مظهریّت و وجود و شهود و مستتبع واحدیّت

و موجودیّت و شاهدیّت و مشهودیّت و همچنین ظهور که

لازم نور است مسبوقت بطون و بطون را تقدّم ذاتی و

اولیّتست نسبت باظهور پس اسم اوّل و آخر و ظاهر و باطن

متعیّن شد همچنین در تجلّی ثانی و ثالث الی ما شاء الله نسب

و اضافات متضاعف می شود و هر چند تضاعف نسب

و اسماء او بیشتر ظهور او بلک خفا او بیشتر فسبحان من احتجب

واطلاق این اسم برحضرت حق سجانه یعنی تائی است نه معنای اول

پس بی قیاس بعقل اصحاب نمود	جز عارض غیب رجای و نمود
لیکن بمکاشفات ارباب شهود	اعیان همه عارضند و مجمر روح

صفات غیر ذاتند من حیث یا بینه العقول

وعین ذاتند من حیث التحقق والحصول مثلاً عالم ذاتست

باعتبار صفت علم و قادر باعتبار قدرت و مرید باعتبار

ارادت و شک نیست که اینها چنانکه بحسب مفهوم ملکدم

متغایر ندم ذات را نیز مغایر ندا ما بحسب تحقق وهستی

عین ذاتند بآن معنی که آنجا وجود ات متعدد نیست بلکه

وجود یست واحد و اسماء و صفات نسب و اعتبارات او

ای در همه شان ذات تو پاک آمدن	فی درحق کعبه تو ان کنت این
از روی تفصل همه غیر ند صفات	باذات تو و ز روی تحقق عین

ذات همه جزء و جو د و قایم بوجود ... ذات تو وجود و سادج هستی

بس بی زنگشت یار دلخواه ای ... قانع نسوی بزرگ ناگاهی دل

اصیل همه زکماه ازان بلی هست ... من احسن صنعته من اللهی دل

لفظ وجود راکه معنی تحقق وحصول که معانی

مصدریه و مفهومات اعتباریه اذا اطلاق میکنند وبدان

اعتبار ازقبل معقولات ثانیه است که در برابر وی امری

نیست درخارج بلکه ما بیاب راعارض میشود در تعقل

چنانک تحقیقان حکماء ومکلمین حسین آن کرده. اندوکه بلفظ وجود

میکویند وحقیقتی میخوامند که هستی وی قلذات خودست

وهستی باقی موجودات بوی وی آنچه به غیر ازوی موجودی نیست

درخارج وباقی موجودات عارض وبند وقایم بوی چنانک

ذوق کل کبراء عارفین وعظماء اهل یقین بان کواهی میدهد

عمر جاوِدانی صرف آن نسبت کند هیچ مکرد و باشد

وحق آن کاپنهی حب ی نیاورده

برعودِدلِ نواخت کیت نغمهٔ عشق	زان نغمهٔ ام زبای تا سرِ عشق
حقا که بعبد ها نایم سپرون	اعهده حق گزاری کرده عشق

حقیقت حق سبحانه و خربستنی نیست و هستی اورا

انخلاط و هستنی نی مقدست انیست تبدل و تغیّر و مبرّاست

از وصمت تعدّد و کثرا ز همه نشانهای نشان نه درعلم خجد

و نه درعیان همه جندها و چونها از و پدا و اوبی چند

وچون همه چزها با و مدرک وا و از احاطهٔ ادراک

برون چشم سرّ درمشاهدهٔ جمال او خیره و ببدهسر

ستنے ملاحظِ کمال او تیره.

| یا من لها وکت بالسجوحت | سم فوقی بهم تحت نه فوقی وه |

دوام این نسبت از وی و شوا رسپت اما چون با ریضتا
لطف درونی ظهور کند و مشغله محسوسات و معقولات را
از باطن وی دور و التذاذ بان غلبه کند بر لذات جسمانی برآنگا
روحانی کلفت مجاهده از میانه برخیزد و لذت مشاهده
در جانش آویزد خاطر از مزاحمت اغیار بپردازد زبان
حالش بدین ترانه ترنم آغاز نهد

| وی با یه غم نیست زیاد تو را | کای دل جان مست نیست بادا تو را |
| ذوقی که د مد و نیست زیاد تو را | لذات جهان را همه در پیش کند |

چون طالب صادق مقدمه نسبت جذبه را که
التذاذ نیست با دکرو حق تسبیحانه درخود بازیابد می باشد
که تمامی همت را بر ترتیب و تقویت آن کار د و از هر چه
مبانی آنست خود را باز دارد روحانیان اند که اکرم المشل

از قبیل ماسوی جهد سبحانه پس شور زبان فنائی فنا باشد

از خرمن مستیت جوی کاهی	زنسان که بقای خویشتن بسجوئی ...
کردم زنبی از ره فناکرامی	تا کیسه موز خویش اگر آستی ...

توحید یگانه گردانیدن دلست یعنی تخلیص و تجرید

او از تعلق ما سوی حق سبحانه هم از روی طلب و ارادت

وهم از رهبت علم و معرفت یعنی طلب و ارادت او از همه

مطلوبات و مرادات منقطع گردد و همه معلومات و

معقولات از نظر بصیرت او مرتفع شود از همه روی

توجه کرده اند و بغیر از حق سبحانه آگاهی و شورش نماند

نخلیص دل از توجه او پت بغیر	توحید پوزف صوفی ای صاحب بصیر
کنم بتوکر فهم کنی منطق طیر	دمری ز نهایات مقامات طیور

مادام که آدمی مبام سوا و سوس کفایت

آن نسبت قوی ترک کوشش می باید کرد تا خواطر متفرقه از

ساحت سینه جمله بیرون رانده و نور ظهور هستی حق سبحانه بر

باطن پرتو افکنده ترا از نیستی باز ستاند و از مزاحمت اغیار برهاند

نیشوری بخود دت ماند و نیشعور بعدم شعور بل امست الا الله او احد الا حد

یا رب ابتدای گر ز دنج در بهم	از بی سبب مرم و ز بدی خود در بهم
در هستی خود مرا زخود بخود کن	تا از خودی و بخودی خود دبیرهم
انراکه فنا شیوه و فقر است امن آن	ای کشف و یقین نه معرفت تست د
رفت او ز میان چه مین جدا ماند خدا	الفقراذا تم هواالله نیست

فنا عبارت از آنست که بواسطه استیلای ظهور

هستی حق بر باطن ما سوی او نیشور نماند و پوشیده نباشد کفنا

فنا در فنا مانند رحمت زیرا که صاحب فنا را اگر بقای خود نیشور

بد صاحب فنا نباشد بلکه آنک صفت فنا و موصوف آن

در هیچ وقتی از اوقات وحالتی از حالات ازان منسبت

خالی نباشی چه در آمدن ور فتن و چه در خوردن و خفتن

وچه در نشستن وگفتن و بالجمله در جمیع حرکات و سکنات

حاضر وقت می باید بود تا بطالت بکذر دلیک

واقف نفس باشی تا بغفلت بنماید

حاشا که بود مهر ترا وبیم زوال	نخ گرچه نمی نمایم سال سال
در دل ز تو آرزو و در دیده خیال	وار مهمه جا بابنه کسر دربه حال

چنانکه امتداد نسبت مذکور رجب تحول

جمیع اوقات وازمان واجبت همچنین از دنیا دکیفیت ان

بسبب تعری از ملابسه اکوان و تبری از ملاحظه صور امکان

اتم مطالبست وآن خبر جهدی بلمغ وجدی تمام هیچ نقص خولطر

واو بام میسر نکرد در جهت خواطر مشغی ترو سادس مختنی تر

اقبال کنی وحقیقتی اشتغال نمایی که در جات موجودات بهمهجا

جمال ایند ومراتب کاپنات مرایی کمال او وبرین نسبت

چندان مداومت نمای که با جان تو درآمیزد وهستی توناظر

تو برخیزد اگر بخود روی آوری روی با وآورده باشی وچون

از خود تعبه کنی تعبیر از وکرده باشی تمهید مطلق شود وما الحق تمو الحق

گرد ر دل تو گل گذر دل باشی	وربلبل معتبر از ببل باشی
توجز و ی وتق گلست اگر روزی	الیش گل مشبه کنی گل باشی
زا پیر کش جان ق تن توهی مقصودم	وز مردن وریستن قهی مقصودم
تو دیر بزی که من رهستم دنیا	گرمن گویم زمن توستی مقصودم
ی با بند گی لباس هستی شدیق	با بان گشته جمال وجه مطلق
دل د ر سطوات نور او مستهلک	جان در غلبات شوق او مستعر

و رز نشان نسبت شعر یقه می با بد کرد بر وجهی که

آدمی اگر چه بسبب جسمانیت ودرغایت کثافت

اما الحبب روحانیت ودرنهایت لطافتست   بہر چه روی

آرد حکم ان کیرد و بہر چه توجه کند زنک آن نپذیرد ولهذا

حکما کفته اند چون نفس ناطقه بصور مطابق حقایق متجلی شود

وباکام صادق آن متحقق کردد صارت کانها الوجو دکله

وایضاً معوم خیالاتی بواسطه شدت اقبال ہمین صورت

جسمانی وکمال اشتغال من بیکر مولانی جان شده اندخوذرا

ازان بازنمی دایند وامتیاز نمی توانند دفی المثنوی المولوی قد تسم

کر کلیت اندیشه تو کلشنی ‖ ور بو د خاری تو ہیمه ی کلخنی

بس با بدک کبویشی دخو درا از نظر خو دبپوشی ودربدانی

جمیل علی الاطلاق ذوالجلال والافضال است

هر جمال و کمال که در جمیع مراتب ظاهرست پرتو جمال و کمال

اوست آنجا یافته و ارباب مراتب بدان سمت

جمال و صفت کمال یافته هر کرا انایی دانی اثر دانایی

اوست و هر کجا بینایی شنیدنی ثمره بینایی اوست

و به آیینه همه صفات اوست از اوج کلیت و اطلاق شل

فرموده و در حضیض جزویت و تقیید تجلی نموده تا توان

جزو کل را ه بری و از نقید به اطلاق روی آوری ند آنک

جزو از کل ممتاز داریمی و مقید از مطلق بازدانی

چون دیدم میان گلشن گفتم بناز	رقم نمای کل آن شمع طراز
از اصل و گلهای حسن میناز	من اصلم و گلهای حسن فرعم
وزیلسله زلف مجعد حکینی	از لطف قد و صباحت خد

بپست آمال وامانی چو دی وپشت اعتماد بدین فرخر فا

فانی چه پنے دل از ہمہ برکن و در خدای بند و از ہمہ گل

و باخدای مو ند   او سپت کہ ہمیشہ بو د و ہمیشہ باشد

و چہرہ بقایش را خار ہیبے حاد ثہ نخراشد

مصورت دلکش تر ا روئی د	خواہد فلکش نہ و در چشم تو برود
رفت آنکہ بقبلہ تبان و لی آرم	دل بے کیے د ہ کہ در اطوار بود و خود
اہنگ جمال جاو و دانی ام	حرف غمشان موج دل گام
چیزی کہ نہ روی در بقا بستے از و	چینی کہ نہ جاودان از ان پذیرم
از ہر چہ بمرد کی جدا خواہی شد	آخر ہدف تیر فنا باستے از و
ای خواجہ اگر مال اگر و زر یست	آن بہ کہ بزندگی جدا نائی از و
خوش آکہ دلش بدلبری درست	سپ داست کہ مدت بقایش جہ
	کشن ا دل و جان ا ہل لست تو ید

حق سبحانه وتعالی همه جا حاضر است و در همه

حال بظاهر و باطن همه ناظر است زبی خبارت که تو

دیده از لقای او برداشته سوی دیگر نگری و

طریق رضای او گذاشته راه دیگر سپری

گفت ای زتو بر خاطر من گران	آمخ سرآن ز لب خونین جگران
باشم تو نی چشم سوی دگران	شهر مت باد که من سوی نگران
وصل تو جدِ جبر خوبان عمر	یابم براه عشق پویان عمر
بهتر که جمال خوب رویان همه عمر	یک چشم زدن خیال تو نقش نظر

ماسوی حق عز و علا در معرض زوال است وفنا

حقیقتش معلوم است معدوم وصورتش موجود لیس موسوم

دی روزنه بود داشت و ننمود وامروزنمود لیس

نی بود و پیداست که فردا ازوی جبه خواهد کشود زمان انقیاد

با امور متعدد پراکنده سازی و جمعیت آنکه از همه مشابه؟

واحد پردازی جمعی کان نزد که جمعیت درجمع اسباب

در ثغره ابد ماند فرقه سقین دانست که جمع اسباب

از اسباب ثغره است دست از همه افشانند

مشکل شو از مشکل زهمه آسوده تر دل زهمه	ای در دل تو هزار مشکل زهمه
دلرا بکی سپار و بکل زهمه	چون ثغره دلت حاصل آمد
در مذهب اهل حق جمع سراسے	مادام که در تفرقه و بپوا
انسانی بے خود در جبل بے تماشے	لا والله ناهس نفس ناسے
جز راه وصول رب ارباب مجوی	ای سالک رنج به رهاب یکی
جمعیت دل زجمع اسباب مجوی	چون علت ثغره است اسباب جهان
تکمیل اصول و حکمت و هندسه	ای دل طلب کمال در مدرسه
شه می زخرد ابدا را بین پوسیده	هر فکر که جز ذکر خدا ابد سوده است

در عالم قرب نشانی اولی *** در قصهٔ عشق زبانی اولی

تا مگر که نه اهل ذوق اسرار بود *** گفتن طبرستی ترجمانی اولی

شمع که چند خور و شمع خبردان *** در ترجمه حدیث عالی سندان

باشد ز من هیچ مدان مصدان *** این تحفه رسانند نشان بدان

جَعَلَ مَا جَعَلَ اللّٰهُ لِرَجُلٍ مِنْ قَلْبَیْنِ یُحْضَرُتُ چون

که ترا نعمت بسی داده است *** در درون تو خبر یک دل

نهاده است تا در محبت او یکرو باشی و یک دل واز

غیر او معرض و بر و مقبل نه الکک یک دل را بصد پاره

کنی و صد پاره را در پی مقصدی و آواره سینه

ای آنکه نقله و فارو است ترا *** بر مغز چرا حجاب شد دوست ترا

دل درین آن و آن نیکو است ترا *** یک دل داری مست یک دوست ترا

تفرقه عبارت از آنست که دل را بواسطهٔ تعلق

یارب بر باییم زحرمان چه شود   رابی دهیم کوی عرفان چه شود

غم کبر که از کرم مسلمان کوی   یک کبر که کر کنی مسلمان چه شود

یارب ز دو کون بی نیازم کردان   وز افسر فقر سرفرازم کردان

در راه طلب محرم رازم کردان   زان ره که زسوی تست بازم کردان

این رساله است مستی بالواح در بیان معارف

و معانی که بر الواح اسرار و ارواح ارباب عرفان واصحاب

ذوق و وجدان لایح کشته بعبارات لایقه و اشارات رایقه

متوقع که وجود متصدی پی این پا زا در میان نه بهند و بر بساط

اعراض و سماط اعتراض بنشینند چه ا در ا درین کفت وکوی

نصیبی خرمنصیب ترجمانی بی وبهره غیرا زشیوه سخن لبانی بی

من بهم و کم ترهینج هم سازی   ازبنج و کم ازهینج نیاید کار

مرسر که زاسیرا زحقیقت کوم   زانم بنود دهره بجبر کشاری

ماکجای و مرچیز راخپا که هست با نمای هستی رابرما در

صورت مستی جلوه مده . . . از هستی برجمال هستی پرده منه

این صُورخیالی را آئینه تجلیات جمال خود گردان علّت

حجاب و دوری وز این نقوش بهی راسرمایه دانایی و بینایی

ماگردان نه آلت جهالت و کوری و محرومی و مهجوری ما

همه از ماست مارا بجما کذار مارا از ما رهایی کرامت

کن و با خود آشنایی ارزانی دار

آن شب وکریه سحرکامم »»	یارب دل پاک و جان کلیم ده »
آنکه خود زخود به خود دراهم »»	در راه خود اول خودم خودکن »

وز جمله جانیان مرا کیست بکن	یارب همه خلق را ایمن بخوکن
و درعشق خود نمک کبت ویک روکن	روی دل من صرف کن از هر جهتی

جایی که زبان آور آنا افصح علم فصاحت اذاخته وخودرا

در ادای ثنای بوعاجز شناخته شکسته زبانی راچه امکان

زبان کشایی و مرآ شفه رایی راچه یارای سخن آرایی لیک آنجا

اظهار اعتراف بعجز و قصور عین قصور است و بآن سرور

دین بدوی دین معنی مشارکت حست ازحسن ادب دور

ما مپسری سکانش با شنویم	من کیستم اندر چه شمارم کنم
این پس که رسید زدوراپگ حبسم	در قافله که او ست دانم زنم

اللهم صل علی محمد ناصیب لواء الحمد و صاحب المقام المحمود

وعلی اله واصحابه الفایزین بنیل المجود دنیل المقصود و سلم تسلیما

آلهی آلهی خلصنا عن الاشتغال بالملاهی

وارنا حقایق الأشیاء کما هی غشاء الغفلت از بصر بصیرت

لا اُحصى ثناءً علیک کیف و کلّ ثناءٍ یعود الیک جلّ عن
ثنایی جناب قدسک انت کما اثنیت علی نفسک ٭ خداوندا

سپاس تو بر زبان نمی آریم و ستایش تو بر تو نمی شماریم
هر چه در صحایف کاینات از جنس اثنیه و محامد ست همه
بجناب عظمت و کبریای تو عاید ست ٭ از دست و زبان
ما چه آید که سپاس و ستایش تو را شاید ٭ تو جنابِ خود
کفهٔ ٭ و گو هر ثنای تو آنست که خود گفتهٔ

آنجا که کمال کبریای تو بود	عالم سینه از بحر عطای تو بود